PRAISE FOR FROM GRIEF TO GRACE

Authentic. Raw. Hopeful. Grief is such a sensitive, tender topic and one that brings up a lot of pain. *From Grief to Grace* is a book that shares vulnerability about loss and disappointment while offering hope and healing. Thank you, Julie, for this gift. May your words and stories be a testimony to those walking through a hard season.

— BETH GUCKENBERGER, AUTHOR, SPEAKER, CO-EXECUTIVE DIRECTOR AT BACK2BACK MINISTRIES

Rarely will you find an author with as much credibility as Julie Maguire on the topic of her book *From Grief to Grace*. I have personally watched Julie live through more grief in the last 16 years than most people experience in a lifetime. With an unrelenting faith in God, in seasons of loss and suffering, Julie gives hope, honesty, and the credibility of someone who's lived through it and seen the light of God's love and grace not just at the end of the tunnel, but in it. This is a great resource for anyone who's walking through a season of grief. As a pastor, I will use it often.

— PASTOR PAUL TAYLOR, LEAD AND FOUNDING PASTOR AT RIVERS CROSSING CHURCH, CINCINNATI, OH

For those struggling with loss, *From Grief to Grace* puts words to the unexplainable, provides hope for despair, and practical strategies to help you cope. This honest and vulnerable examination of grief is a helpful guide, written by someone who has walked in your shoes. This story is full of wisdom, delivered in a way that will impact you immediately. You'll find yourself smiling, crying, and experiencing hope again!

— BRETT DOWDY, PSY.D., CHIEF OF
PSYCHOLOGICAL SERVICES AT LINDNER
CENTER OF HOPE

A real-life look into the grieving journey. This book takes a difficult topic and not only makes it relatable but gives hope that there is healing through the process. We don't move on, we move forward, and this book is an excellent insight into what that can look like.

— DANIEL COWAN MA, LPC

Julie writes about her very personal journey after the death of my brother, Charley, with candor, courage, and compassion, both for herself and for others facing similar journeys.

— ALICE HARTMANN DAVIS

FROM GRIEF TO GRACE

A WOMAN'S STORY OF LOVE, LOSS & THE
CHALLENGE OF ONCE AGAIN EMBRACING
GOD'S HEALING

JULIE MAGUIRE

HawkSong
PUBLICATIONS

From Grief to Grace: A Woman's Story of Love, Loss & the Challenge of Once Again Embracing God's Healing

Copyright © 2024 by Julie Maguire
Published by HawkSong Publications (Colorado)

Cover by Madelyn Copperwaite, MC Creative LLC
Editing by Jennifer Crosswhite, Tandem Services Ink
Layout by Stephanie Feger, emPower PR Group

First edition, April 2024
ISBN: 979-8-2183624-5-4
Library of Congress Control Number: 2024903118
Created in the United States of America

Learn more about Julie Maguire and reach out to inquire about securing her for speaking engagements at julie-maguire.com. Special discounts are available on quantity book purchases as well.

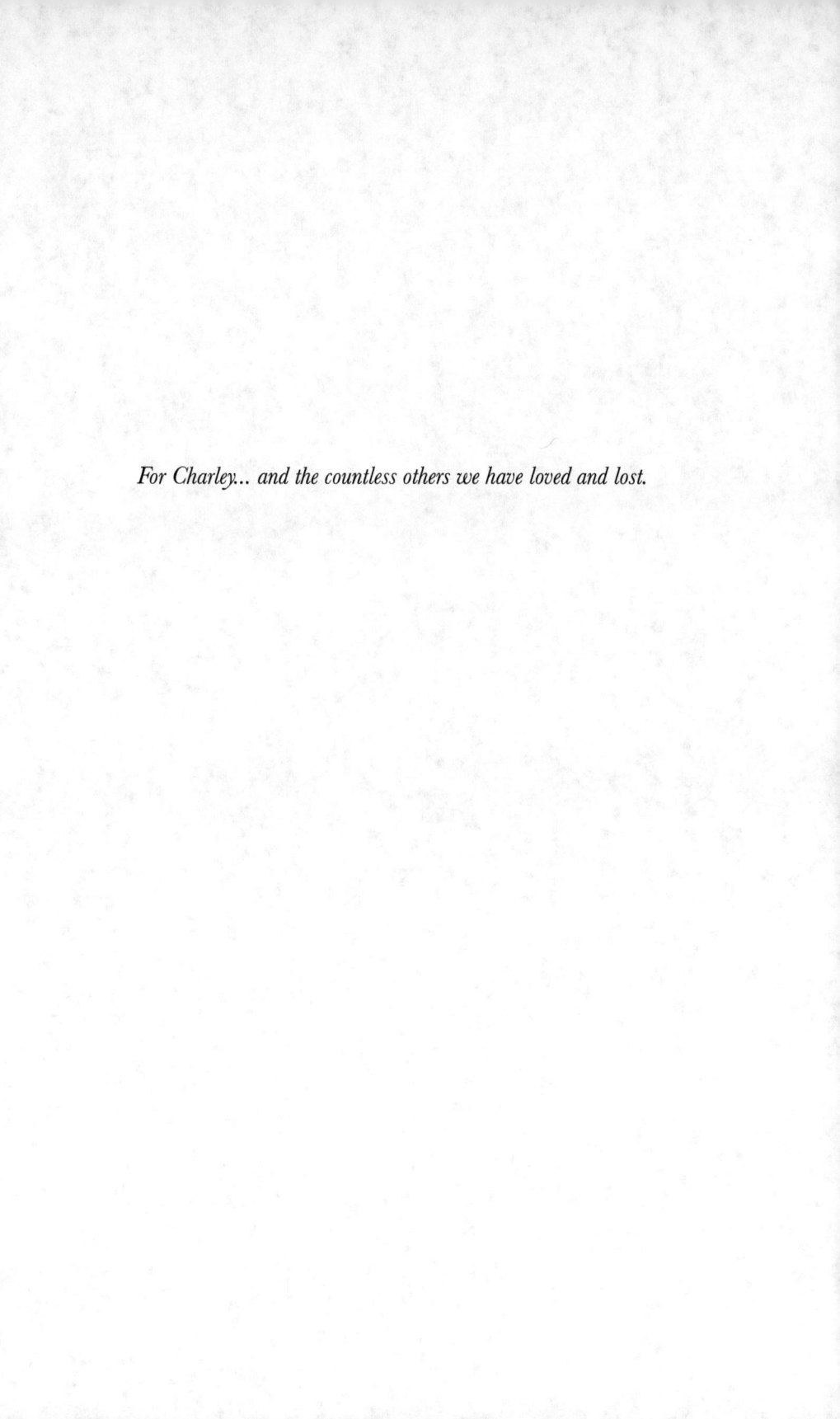

For Charley... and the countless others we have loved and lost.

TABLE OF CONTENTS

LETTER TO THE READER

Hello, my name is Julie Maguire; my friends and family call me JuJu. If you are here, I consider you part of that group. It's nice to meet you.

Because you are reading my story, I am going to assume you or someone you love has experienced a loss in your life. If you're currently experiencing grief or have in the past, you know it can rob you of your joy and make you feel paralyzed in a world that seemingly continues to revolve without you. So, as we embark on this journey of healing together, I simply want to say: *I'm so very sorry for your loss.*

These are the only words I am confident in and will say directly to you today without knowing your story. Grief is different for everyone, and pain levels vary. As I have navigated loss in my life in many forms and with many people, I have come to realize that there is nothing I or anyone else can say to make things better, so expressing sincere sorrow seems like the only best option.

Grief is heartbreaking. It's uncomfortable, and it is awkward. Be assured there will be no sugar-coating, random opinions, cliché sayings, or overly spiritual comments from me about your loss. They don't help, and I won't trivialize your pain in that way. Grief sucks.

When I Started Feeling the Push to Write About My Grief, I Thought It Was Just for Myself

I had a desire to record and process my own pain, but as I began to write, I was reminded of how important it is to share with others who feel alone, stuck, or without direction, as I did. I know how important it is to feel community; there are so many unanswered questions in grief, and I find it helpful to speak these things out loud with others. We are all thinking lots of strange things anyway, so let's just say it all out loud. *Why God? What do I do now? What's next? Why did this happen? What the *^&^!* God?*

I'm in no way claiming this book will answer those questions for you, but maybe it will help. I have found that books can be very helpful. But in my early grief, I found reading for long periods of time especially difficult. I was not thinking clearly, and I didn't want or wasn't able to find the energy to read long, over-complicated books on grief. People are so thoughtful and sent me many books, but I found it overwhelming, so I decided to make this book shorter and a real-time account of what I was experiencing. Maybe I could have read a book like this early in my grief; I'm not sure. What I am sure of is that writing it was helpful for me. I hope reading it is for you.

As I began my path to writing this book, my fiancé, Charley, had only been dead for two months. I say dead instead of the many euphemisms we so often use because *I* have to. It's important to me to remind myself of this truth. He hasn't "gone somewhere better" and he wasn't "lost." I understand that it may feel softer and gentler to say things like that, but for me, at least right now, I must keep speaking the truth out loud. I don't want to believe it's true, but it is.

He is dead.

I believe that no matter the loss we face, it's important to give it full terrible credit where terrible credit is due. Inside, we want to run from it, but *procrastination will only prolong the pain.*

We Are All on an Unwanted Journey

We are on an uncharted voyage like Gilligan, and the storm is just starting. We will often feel like we are stranded on a deserted island. We will have days we feel like we get some relief, maybe even feel hope of rescue, only to realize we are still stuck on this godforsaken island with no end in sight. We didn't book this trip, but the voyage is ours. We didn't get to choose what happened, but we do get to choose how we respond to what happened. At least there's that.

So, I'm calling my unwanted trip a journey from *grief to grace*. My hope is that we can take this journey together. I started this in a state of total despair and now I'm beginning to see glimmers of God's grace again. But the truth of the matter is, I have been and often still am very mad. I'm hurt. I still get angry and aggravated thinking about what happened. What I continue seeking through my grief expedition is a return to grace. Grace for me, grace for others, and finally grace for and from God. I want to return to a place of peace, and I can only find that by once again offering and receiving grace.

So, this book will be a practical, honest, and sometimes a very raw discussion on what grief is and has done to me. I found so many things were so very hard and still can be. I had and still have the desire to talk about them, but I needed to talk to those who understand what the pain feels like in real time. I'm guessing you do too.

Loss doesn't stop life, but it permanently changes it.

Grief stays long after the last hot pasta meal is sent, the flowers wilt, and sympathy cards stop arriving in the mail. People leave, but grief hangs around, right up in your face. It is incurable, not fatal, but it's ours, forever.

For us, the ones left behind, there is absolutely life after death.

In my career as a ministry leader, business owner and peer counselor for mental health and addiction, I've learned and taught about recovering from a variety of hurts, addictions, losses, and traumas. I believe there can be purpose in pain and, additionally, that our greatest ministering and encouragement to others may come from our deepest wound. I have used my negative experiences to help others over time, but when you are in a deep and recent grief situation, it is hard to help yourself, let alone anyone else.

Grief is a monster of its own, and I want to stress how important it is to be aware of how we treat those who are grieving.

We are one of *those*. In my grief, so many said so much, always meaning well and often causing more pain. When grief is fresh, everything feels escalated and personal, even words that people say meaning kindness. I have truly come to believe that less is more. it may be better to simply be present rather than say something to cause harm.

We *can* learn to love each other better during traumatic times. It is simple but is surely not always easy, like so many other things in life. I don't have a quick fix for pain, sorrow, or suffering. This book sure isn't one. No *Grief for Dummies* here. This isn't a self-help instructional book on grief. But I hope to share some of my experience, strength, parts of my pain, and my hope. A hope that there is a meaningful life waiting for us through and after grief. You're not alone, and you *are* going to be okay.

When I was struggling or emotional, Charley would hold my face tightly in his strong hands, look me deep in the eyes, and tell me, "Even though you don't *feel like* it, you're okay. You're going to be okay, babe."

I believed him then, and I refuse to stop believing it now.

A LITTLE MORE ABOUT ME

I grew up in Colorado, the daughter of an alcoholic father. I also struggle with the same disease and pair it with my learned people-pleasing tendencies. I am what I like to call a "raging codependent." As a child, I had the unrealistic hope of *earning* what I perceived as my dad's love through my many accomplishments.

As I grew and aged, I realized I was trying to achieve an impossible task, so I threw in the proverbial towel and followed in his footsteps of addiction. I became an active alcoholic, proceeded to marry an alcoholic, and raised my children while battling these demons over a fifteen-year period.

Even after my dad died drunk at fifty-six, I continued my journey of alcoholism and self-harm. It got so serious that I was hospitalized and feared that the disease of alcoholism would take my life even sooner than it took my dad's. After years of damage to myself and decades of accepting toxic and abusive treatment in relationships, I knew something had to change.

So, at thirty-five years old, I came to a very difficult crossroads. I couldn't imagine my life *without* drinking, but I also couldn't imagine my life while *continuing* to drink. It was a real conundrum.

By the grace of God and programs like Alcoholics Anonymous and Celebrate Recovery, I chose to do the work required and got sober. During the writing of this book, I celebrated twenty years of sobriety, and for that, I am truly grateful.

Since working on my own recovery, I have been a part of various recovery ministries and helped in guiding others to find their own healing.

Healing is complicated and not a one-size-fits-all kind of thing. Addiction, for example, comes in all shapes and sizes and tends to be more of a *symptom* of a deeper issue. It's never just about wanting to use drugs and alcohol or food or sex as a way to cope. We pick our poison, but there is always more to the question of why we take self-harming action in the first place.

Wounds can be deep and old and frankly confusing, so we often seek ways to *feel better* because we feel hopeless or hurt. Grief can affect us in a similar way. We want—we need—relief! Healing can be slow, regardless of how injury is caused. It takes more time to *transform* an emotion, feeling, or state-of-mind into something different, better than we ever expect it to.

I guess you could say I'm a bit of a transformation junkie. For the past twenty years, I've loved seeing people go through the process of healing and transforming, from a place of angst to the newly accepted space of relief, peace, or joy. This happened to me as I worked on the wreckage of my past and learned to love myself differently. This is my hope now, that I can transform once again through the valley of grief to a deeper understanding of a true state of grace.

Through my own recovery, my relationship with God became very real, tangible, and indispensable. It changed everything for me. It became my most important and valued relationship. My relationship with God has shown me how to repair, restore, and maintain healthy relationships with my family and the communities I've worked with.

If you have a higher power different from mine, don't let that deter you from seeing how similar we truly are. I believe when sharing with others, we can find and enjoy the similarities and learn from the differences. When I come across things I don't understand, I may learn even more from those, but if not, I'll allow my healing to happen by seeing the similarities.

After I stopped drinking, I was able to get my life back on track in many ways. I was able to be a better mom, partner, friend, and mentor to others. But there is always more. To find real peace, I had to understand the deep-rooted causes and wounds that led me to drink in the first place. This self-knowledge is vital to anyone's healing. It's important to understand what the heck you need to be healed from.

This applies to grief as well. Processing and sharing give us the *why* and *how* to contribute to this world and, ultimately, we all want a purpose. In grief, it's so vital to hold on to your purpose. It feels like nothing matters when tragedy hits. We can experience a lack of purpose or desire to give up. It's hard to hear but remember: You didn't die; they did.

In this new season of grief, my purpose is an attempt to apply the lessons and experience of my past to my present to help myself and others.

I believe our past can be our superpower when used correctly. My prayer for you is that, if you feel a lack of purpose in your grief, you might find your purpose again as well.

Finally, my deepest hope is that God uses this book to touch and heal our broken hearts. We are different but so alike. Don't forget the next sentence. (Get the highlighter out now.) We are all average humans; not one of us is terminally unique.

Sometimes we exclude ourselves as unworthy or unable or, conversely, better than. This is ego, and it can play tricks on us. Does the voice inside you say, "This might be good for them, but it won't work for me. It never does," or the flip side, "I already know all of this stuff; will it really change anything"? Whatever your inner critic (we all have one) is shouting, let me stop you.

Let's come to an agreement: We are all unique but alike. You are the same flesh, blood, and bone as other humans. God made you; He made me. He loves our uniqueness, yes, but He also loves us equally. We are all lovable and valuable. With a little willingness and some vulnerability, we do get better. We can find relief, so let's hold on to this book and each other and let go of all of the other crap for a minute. Yes, grief sucks, but we are on a journey. A hard journey in hopes of a soft landing. That softness comes from God's grace.

Great job getting this far.
Take a deep breath.
We are in this together.

CHAPTER 1
WE'LL TALK ABOUT IT TOMORROW

Everything we say at funerals should be said at birthday parties instead.
We leave so much love unspoken.
— Madhu, @justmadhu

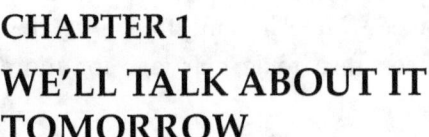hen loss happens—whether it is sudden and shocking, long awaited, or somewhere in between—it can be devastating. Losses may happen differently, but how our bodies react to them tends to be similar. The disbelief. The horror. Typically, our body sends an immediate release of protective hormones to help us cope. Our heart rate changes; our blood flow is affected. We may be disoriented or physically ill for a period of time. In sudden loss, we go into shock, denial, horror; shock, denial horror; repeat.

That's how it was for me around 7 a.m. on Saturday, June 11, 2022. The dreadful morning when the ringing of the doorbell and a repeated heavy knocking on the door woke me up and changed everything.

I was always exhausted on Saturday mornings after a long work week and a busy Friday night at church. I had been out until about ten thirty the night before, like I had been every Friday for the past five and a half years, leading a twelve-step recovery ministry called Celebrate Recovery (CR).

When I was about fourteen years sober, I was serving in a local CR and met a man named Charley. Charles Raymond Hartmann was a gruff character, a big six-foot-five-inch barrel-chested, bald-headed teddy bear. He spoke with an obvious New York accent and was a true blue, blue-eyed, proud Yankees fan. After meeting him, boy, things changed for me! I had been in a toxic marriage for more years than I care to admit.

One thing I have come to understand through my recovery is that *we do the best we can with what we have at the time we have it.*

This concept is vital in forgiveness of ourselves and others. Through a lot of growing up and some hard work, I was finally able to end an unhealthy marriage, and it wasn't long after I became friends with Charley. Not only would Charley show me true love, but he would help me immensely along the next part of my healing journey.

Our relationship began slowly. We had both been divorced recently and had adopted a similar mindset: to live out our future days as happy, single servants of hurting people. Thankfully, someone up above had a different picture of our futures.

My relationship with Charley was beautiful. It was slow-paced, meaningful, and fun. It was all of the things I believed were not ever going to be a reality for me, things happy couples have that I had heard others talk about but never personally experienced. You know, the mushy love stuff.

I was skeptical. I always thought people were actually *mean* and *angry* with each other behind closed doors. That was my experience growing up. That was what I had seen modeled and what had become a reality in my own marriage.

Charley gently held my hand and walked me, very patiently I might add, through a dramatic change of heart and mind. He taught me that it was okay to express my feelings. He encouraged me to tell him what I wanted, needed, and even what I liked or didn't. This was foreign to a people-pleaser such as myself. He gave me permission to be me. He would listen and not try to fix me but instead look at what solutions we could come up with together.

Charley was committed to us having a God-centered relationship in all ways. Even when I was not always patient with him, he would guide me as the loving man I had always dreamed of.

After six months of dating, I finally said to him, "So you gonna kiss me or what?" He gently said, "Why yes, I am. I'm so glad you asked. I've been waiting for you to be ready." It was worth the wait.

Charley came by his wisdom through his earlier years of overcoming drug and alcohol addiction and was devoted to sharing his lessons with me and hundreds of others. Over the years, I have seen that big chunks of knowledge can be helpful, but I believe true wisdom takes root as a person applies that knowledge to their everyday life. Charley walked the walk and the talk.

The night before was a typical Friday night for us. He left Celebrate Recovery early because he had to get up at the crack of dawn Saturday to begin a second career. He had recently retired and was starting as a counselor at a methadone clinic in Cincinnati. He always said, "The more jacked up they are, the better I like working with them." His heart was huge.

Friday nights were always busy for us. Charley led a large group of people, spiritual sons and daughters alike. We were a team, and we always had each other's back in what could prove to be a drama-filled ministry. Earlier in the night, in the chaos of people, I hugged and kissed him like always. (Now, we were that couple!)

I briefly sat with him, touching his face and his beard. I was always telling him how jealous I was of his incredibly soft skin. I looked into his beautiful blue eyes, thinking how much I loved him. He returned my affection and gave me his innocent little crooked smile. That look and that laugh always made my heart leap.

He brought up a ministry concern we needed to discuss, and it was back to reality. As I went my way and he went his, I commented on this concern he had spoken of and said, "Okay, babe. We'll talk about it tomorrow."

Worst Day Ever

When the doorbell rang early Saturday morning, to say I was surprised would be an understatement. First off, no one ever rang my doorbell. If anyone was coming over, I knew they were coming, and I would always leave the door open for them and send a text telling them to come on in. (Honestly, it was because I didn't like going up and down the stairs of my condo to open the door.)

So, when the doorbell woke me that Saturday morning, I almost dismissed it as a neighborhood kid trying to sell mulch for their local football team. No way I was going to get out of bed for that this early. But then came the banging on the door.

I sat up so fast, so surprised; who could be banging at my door this early on a Saturday? I hurried, got on a robe, and approached my stairs. The knocking didn't stop, becoming more persistent the closer I got to the door. I had no idea who it might be.

But once I was down my stairs and took a peek behind my shade-covered window, my heart moved to my throat. There it was, what no one wants to see when they look out the window: two police officers standing on the porch. One had worked security at our meeting the previous night.

I immediately flashed back to a time in my life many years earlier when my son had been in a car accident. I suffer from some post-traumatic stress disorder (or PTSD). Because of my history, some difficult situations can bring me back to places in the past that I pray I can someday forget. We'll talk more about this a little later.

When I saw the officers standing outside my door, it hit me for a split second as if I was standing at the front door of my old home, terrified. Back then, I was looking out a different window at different police officers, feeling the same dread. I was expecting the worst news to be delivered about my son that day. By the grace of God, on that day so many years ago the worst *didn't* happen.

The flashback felt like slow motion, like an eternity, when in reality, only a few seconds had passed. My brain now suddenly and abruptly beamed me back to the present. My mind was racing. I found myself wondering who this could be about, why the police were at my place, and frantically thinking of all the people close to me.

Panic set in, then denial and fear. All I knew to do was pray, "Oh God, no. Please God, not my kids. Oh God, help me. Oh God."

When I opened the door, the officer I knew said, "Julie, go upstairs." I assume he knew this would be my last best chance to physically make the climb upstairs. After delivering whatever terrible information he was about to give me, he must have known I would be too sick to do anything, especially drag my lifeless frame up a hill.

His face said it all, yet I still could not imagine who this was about.

I needed to know one thing right then before attempting to climb the fifteen stairs that appeared like Mount Everest in front of me. "Just tell me, is this local or out of state?"

He said, "It's local."

Still confused, I was able to catch my breath. I guess it's a mother's instinct to think of her children first. This elimination somehow gave me a ten-second reprieve of what I imagined would be my worst-case scenario. *Local* meant all my kids, my mom, and my siblings were okay since they lived in other states.

Nevertheless, I felt great confusion. The rest of my family, all my friends... This couldn't be about them; someone would have just called me. The only thought of Charley at that time was that I needed to call him ASAP to come take care of me.

As I finally made it to my dining room, I turned and looked at my officer friend.

He took a deep breath before speaking. "There was a fire at Charley's house. Julie, he didn't make it out."

Wait. What?! *That's not possible.*

Processing unbelievable news actually feels impossible when it's taking place. A whirlwind of pictures like an old staticky movie clip runs through your mind while you try to understand and make sense of the information just given to you. Your mind can't compute. And then it happens, you receive and understand what has been said to you. Your person is dead.

I've lost many people in my life: family, friends, and acquaintances. I've lost people I loved and mentored in recovery. I've walked with many who have lost children, so much loss. It's honestly hard to put into words or comprehend why I've seen so much loss. My son says I've seen more people die than an ER doctor. Why God had me in all those lives, I don't know. The reality is some things we will not know or understand in this life.

Charley always made it sound so simple when I asked about injustice, loss, and tragedy. He would simply look at me with that grin and baby blues, wink, and say, "You can ask Jesus when you get there, babe. He'll have all the answers." He would giggle, and I would sigh in frustration.

God never said life would be fair. Jesus actually said the exact opposite when He told the disciples about what trials were ahead. He reminded them that He knew His Father would always be with Him even at His lowest but made it crystal clear that this would be hard. "I've told you these things so that you may have peace in me. Here on earth you will have times of trials and sorrow. But take heart, because I have overcome the earth" (John 16:33, NLT).

The knowledge that God won't leave me is comforting. In deep grief it can *feel* as if God has left us. It's okay to feel this way as long as we remember feelings aren't facts.

Jesus gets it. He also felt alone in the garden of Gethsemane and on the cross, just to mention a couple of places. He experienced so much pain on the earth. He literally asked God, "Why have you forsaken me?"

I can relate. But as He did, we can find our comfort once again, in God. We will eventually have peace eternally. As Christians, we believe and this knowledge is the great gift of grace. But in the meantime, we get the privilege of living in this jacked-up place.

For me, when we know someone is dying, having that time with them before they die can be such a gift. You get to say important words if you're able and willing. But no matter how you lose someone, it's always brutal. Your body and mind always feel the immediate pain of knowing that you don't get to talk to, see, or touch this person again on this earth. Ever.

After my uninvited police officer friend said the unwanted, terrible words, it took a minute to register. When I was finally able to hear the words and process the information that Charley was dead, I felt as though I was going to throw up. My body immediately got weak. I had to sit or fall down.

Your body physically responds to grief. You really *are* sick. You may feel like you'll die yourself for the first few minutes. Your heart beats so hard you're certain everyone can hear it. There is a buzz, a ringing in your ears, and nothing makes sense or sounds clear. You hear only the thumping of your own erratic heartbeat pounding in your head. It is truly a dramatic response.

After this experience with Charley, when I see this type of scene in a movie, it affects me very differently. Now I often cry on the spot. Don't be fooled; it's not because the actor deserves an Oscar. It's because I've been there in real, non-theatrical life. It truly is as terrible as they are making it look.

This is why it is important not to judge people's emotional reactions to grief. We can never completely understand why someone is affected the way they are by things that may have no meaning to them. A doorbell ringing, pounding on the door, a movie scene, or a steak at Costco. (Yep, beef brisket does it for me.) These are "triggers" or "stressors," as mental health professionals prefer to call them, which are so very real in grief. It's important not to judge yourself or others.

In these difficult situations we must realize that anyone affected in this way is likely not firing on all cylinders. I know I wasn't. What ensued is all a bit cloudy, but I do remember the officers saying: "Who can we call? You can't be alone." I thank God for the kind men and women doing the difficult job of delivering terrible news on a daily basis.

So now what, Julie? I abruptly came to the realization that I had to not only try to process it myself, but share the information with all the other people.

The officer called Charley's sister Alice. All I remember is the deep agonizing groan that came over the phone as I tried saying the words. I thought Charley would surely want her to be my first call. My thinking was erratic. It was truly a grueling process and one that required help. How do I tell the kids? How could I possibly add another person to the name of loved ones and friends they have lost?

I called people who could call other people. It was one terrible, exhausting, and unbelievable call after the next. I was blessed to have people who just showed up in the midst of the chaos. One after another, they came. One terrible look after look, disbelieving hug after hug. An ongoing combination of crying, disbelief, and breakdowns. It was all so terrible and at the same time, in the darkness of it all, such a beautiful display of God's love in action. People comforting and loving people. I know Charley would have been proud of all of us.

Now some practicality.

Throughout the years, due to the many losses in my immediate family, I felt it was necessary to establish some preventative actions. I call these actions **Life Clauses**.

With the losses we have experienced, my kids and I have become sensitive to certain things that can cause PTSD or trigger unrealistic emotions. So, we decided to put into practice some specific applications to help us cope and communicate. I'm giving you practicality because it is important to have action steps in our healing.

Phone Call Clause

Something that causes anxiety is unexpected late-night calls or cryptic texts. During my kids' high school and college years, we lived in a county in middle-class Ohio that regularly ranked in the top three in the nation for opioid deaths. We lost so many friends and children of friends during this period. Every time one of us would call for whatever reason, our first initial reaction would be to assume something bad happened. And so, something simple like answering the phone became a trigger. Let's be honest, we mostly texted, so when we *did* call, it was already not typical.

In order to alleviate unwarranted stress, we implemented the "everything is okay" phone call clause.

For my family, something as simple as starting the conversation by saying, "Hi, everything is okay," has become an easy solution. We don't send texts or leave a voicemail that says, "Call me." We let the person know all is well prior to any other information.

When I called my kids to tell them about Charley, they immediately knew it was serious because I said, "Everything's **not** okay." From there, you do your best to make sure they are in safe a place (not driving) and attempt to proceed with your catastrophic news.

This small step helps us avoid unnecessary post-traumatic anxiety. Post-traumatic stress disorder or PTSD is defined by Webster as a condition of persistent and emotional stress occurring as a result of injury or severe psychological shock. Losing someone you love suddenly is absolutely a severe psychological shock.

I Love You Clause

For Charley, tomorrow never came. I remember my last words to him so vividly: "We'll talk about it tomorrow." It haunted me at first. I stewed about that for some time. "Really Julie," I would say to myself. "That's the last thing you told the man you loved before he died?" Well, yes it was.

Of course, I didn't know he was going to die. So, I have to stop picking on myself! Are you picking on you? I want to ask you to stop if you are. There are plenty of others who will do that to you sufficiently. You don't need to add to the dysfunction here. Remember, *you did the best you could with what you had at the time.*

A very practical life clause we use is simply the words: "I love you." We say it relentlessly. We say it often and mean it every time. I try to make sure it's the last words anyone I love hears when parting. I never want to regret not saying those three simple little words. The last words I said to my dad on the phone were, "I love you." He did not reciprocate, but it doesn't matter, because it was for me, not him. He died that same night.

I say I love you frequently, even if it's with someone I may not "like" a great deal at the moment. (Let's be honest. We don't like everyone 24/7!) This can be especially true with family, but that is not an excuse not to love. God asks us often in Scripture to love one another. It's not just a request but, in fact, a commandment. Jesus says in John 13:34 (ESV), "A new commandment I give to you, that you love one another: just as I have loved you, you also are to love one another." It's not rocket science or a surprise that we are to be loving. Thankfully, there is no Scripture saying, "Thou shalt *like* each other all of the days of ye life."

Because we are humans with active and intelligent brains, we have the ability to *choose* to love regardless of how we feel. Feelings can be very unreliable. Feelings are not facts. You can choose to show love with your words and actions, even when you kinda wanna throat punch someone.

There is a Garth Brooks song called *If Tomorrow Never Comes*. It always makes me consider my love and treatment of others when I hear it. Have I tried to show love in every way I could? If tomorrow truly never came, how would I feel about how I treated that person? When I had to contemplate this for Charley, it took on an even deeper burden inside my heart. Contemplating the question "Did I try and show?" was heartbreaking and painful but necessary. Try and show; they are action words. Love is proactive. Love is a decision. We must make up our minds to think about this while we are still here and able to actively love.

Deciding to relentlessly love now, helps us avoid regret later.

Love more, regret less.

Still, as much as I've committed to never part ways with someone I love without telling them so, it isn't foolproof. Life is busy, and we are often in a hurry. Life happens, and people die suddenly. We are not promised tomorrow.

I had to come to terms with the fact that "I love you" wasn't the last thing I said to Charley. I know he knew, and I am thankful we had a healthy relationship in which we told each other of our love every day. But it still hurts. Never in a million years did I think that Friday evening would be the last time I would ever see him. The words, "We'll talk about it tomorrow" sting.

I assumed we would actually talk about it, all of it, tomorrow.

Will tomorrow be soon enough? We can never know. That is the reason I must focus on doing what I can each day. Living in the present, *one day at a time,* may sound cliché, but I have found this simple concept a very important tool for living a more peaceful life. So *just for today,* let's agree to express our love to those who matter the most to us.

I challenge you to start practicing the *I love you* clause when you part ways with those you love. Maybe even sit and discuss this action step with your family and agree to be intentional by putting it into practice. It's a great way to show love and appreciation for each other. Heck, you may even see some improvement in your relationships after you decide to enact this simple but very powerful tool. Give it a shot; I have faith in you.

You've read a lot. Grief is exhausting. Feel free to put the book down and reflect, and if you're up to it, why not make a call? (If you just can't stand it, feel free to read on.) Who do you need to or just want to tell I love you right now? Go ahead and make it happen.

Oh, and before you go, I love you.

> *Love is patient and kind. Love is not jealous or boastful or proud or rude. It does not demand its own way. It is not irritable, and it keeps no record of being wronged. It does not rejoice about injustice but rejoices whenever the truth wins out. Love never gives up, never loses faith, is always hopeful, and endures through every circumstance.*
> 1 Corinthians 13: 4-8 (NLT)

CHAPTER 2
IT'S NOT REALLY
ABOUT THE DISHES

I'm unsure which pain is worse—the shock of what happened or the ache for what will never be.
— Unknown

The latest statistics show that a hundred percent of people living today have a hundred percent chance of dying. Cool. So what do I do now? I imagine I'm not the first person to ask this question after a loss. It's all so confusing, this gambit of emotions, this laundry list of things to do.

In the first week after Charley died, I felt as if I had become a human-doing instead of a human-being. (Charley accused me of being a human-doing often). For someone like me, however, keeping busy seems to help... until it doesn't. Busyness or neglecting my needs for other's needs has been a coping tool for me all of my life. Emotional "doing" kept me occupied and in good old-fashioned denial for a minute after this loss.

But what about after the initial chaos ends? The planning, the services, and the get-togethers all come to what I can only describe as a hard stop. What about after all of the irritatingly normal humans go back to their irritatingly normal lives and irritatingly act as if nothing happened? It's so irritating.

Everything got quiet. People had to go home, back to work, back to their own lives and realities. It got very quiet very quickly and when it did, I couldn't bear to be alone with my own thoughts.

So again, I asked, "What now God?" I felt mad at and completely disconnected from God and, of course, my own life. Everything was different in the blink of an eye.

As I was forced to spend time with my own mind, I grasped at things that had helped me process emotions and pain in the past. I talked to people and, yes, did all I could to stay in the community, but it was exhausting. Coming up with things to say to people was hard in my grief because even speaking felt overwhelming. Grieving takes so much energy, and I just didn't have anything left for anything else.

I realized journaling had helped me in the past. It was one way I could express myself truthfully and cry out to God while not having to expend too much energy holding a conversation with a real person. I could also start and stop whenever I wanted, with no need to explain myself. The day Charley died, I tried to write something on a page at the end of the day. It was hard, and it didn't feel real. It felt like I was writing fiction novel.

You died today. I don't understand how this could be true. It makes me want to break shit, scream, curse the Lord. I do not know what to do. How am I supposed to do this without you?

I didn't feel like journaling. I still often don't. But feelings are sneaky and dishonest. One solution I am a fan of is called "opposite action." Doing the opposite of what I *feel* like doing.

When I don't want to do something, it's often because I have some kind of fear. A negative feeling is telling me I *should be* worried, scared, or angry. I don't want to face these devastating feelings. Fear is a liar, and it's our enemy. Unfortunately, fear is also very good at its job.

To overcome my own fear, I must be aware of negative self-talk and be deliberate about what actions I want to take. When we ask ourselves to do hard things, it is not necessarily done by overcoming our fear. Often it's doing the hard things in spite of it. Healthy people do scary things every day. We are human, and fear is a prominent and consistent feeling. Once we learn and believe that feelings are not facts, we can do things and become brave more often. We can take the opposite action of what fear is telling us.

Journaling felt like one of these scary things after Charley died. It feels scary even now because it brings hurtful things up. It can be painful and raw. I still get angry, and I cry a lot. But I decided to journal and see if it helped.

Healing is a direct result of the work we are willing to do.

This work I do, good or bad, it's mine. I get to choose what direction my grief is headed. I want to focus on forward motion. We all have a pace. Mine will be mine and yours will be yours. But I want my *pace to grace* to be a forward motion.

When you're hurting, it's good to get out of the house, if you can. There were many days when I couldn't, and some I maybe shouldn't have. One particular day my family took me to a water park called The Land of Illusion. In a grief state, you don't always know why, when, or where your emotions will decide to show up. They can sneak up like a lion on the prowl, and when they reveal themselves unannounced, sometimes it's just too late to stop them from taking a bite.

The Land of Illusion

My sister and son took me to a water park today. My son's friends from childhood were there; it was good to see them. My friend, Julie, was there too, so we got to hang out. It was lucky for me that she was there because I unexpectedly verbally assaulted a very nice family on vacation.

Let me explain.

On this particular day, I went with my sister and son. I didn't feel good in my head, but I could either spend another day inside crying or get out and maybe even have some fun. Don't push yourself here. I think I went too far too soon. Do not feel pressured to get back out there before you are ready.

I love the water; so I thought, what harm could it do?

We arrived early, and I reserved two cabanas. You know, something sweet and romantic, like in a movie. Something you would find on a nice beach setting with a lounge chair, palm trees, and coconuts. I put some of my things on the chairs to reserve them for later since I wanted to have a place for my son and his childhood friends who hadn't arrived yet. These kids always brought my momma's heart joy and I was looking so forward to spending time with them.

I needed a reprieve. A reprieve from chaos and pain just for a day, but I already had an air of frustration hovering over me. I couldn't verbalize exactly how I was feeling except for the pain from that one thing: Charley's dead.

By now the place was getting crowded, and I was seeing random people act as if they would sit at one of my *already paid for* and *reserved* cabanas. I would quickly flash them my stink eye and motion for them to move on along. One man tried to use it to protect his computer bag from the sun while he went in the water. I explained I had paid for it, and I would rather he didn't. He wasn't happy with me, but honestly, I didn't give a flyin' fig tree on that particular day.

I was already feeling irrational. I proceeded to the water and enjoyed a little sun. Water is healing to me; I was good. It felt nice.

When I got out of the pool, I headed toward my cabana. To my utter shock and growing disbelief, I saw a family sitting in my spot! A whole family sitting at *my* extra cabana. What the what? Without thought or reason, I made a beeline straight to them. There was no forethought, no pause, just an on-purpose, irrational pace, headed nowhere near grace. I went straight up to what appeared to be the dad of this rude crew, and I immediately opened my mouth. I was that lion, full of grief, and unexplained anger. I had no control over my bite at this point.

The words just came out: "Did you guys move my stuff? Did you actually move *my* stuff? I paid for this cabana, and you just move my stuff and sit here?"

The father looked at me and said calmly, at first, "We didn't move any bags, and we've been here since early morning. I think you're mistaken because *I* paid for this spot." He said this nicely at this point and was still seated, but I was not having it.

I would get my cabana back, and I would prove that these people posing as a nice family on vacation were liars! I reiterated that they needed to give me back my cabana!

The tension was building as the father now stood up in shock and disbelief at what he was seeing and hearing. I had literally puffed my chest and was not budging or shutting up. As they pleaded their case, I finally said, "I'm getting the manager."

His only response was: "Please do, lady!"

Just about the time I was going to get a manager, I glanced to the right and saw my sister waving her hands frantically in the air at me, motioning for me to come to her. I suddenly realized that next to her, right there in plain view, was my other cabana. It was just sitting there, empty.

Pure and utter humiliation. Grief is like that.

I'm grateful to have acquired some tools for making amends from my years of recovery. I attempted to make an apology, not once but twice. The damage, however, had been done. First, I apologized right then and there. I simply stopped, took a deep breath, knelt down, and said, "I am truly so sorry. I've lost my mind. Forgive me." And I walked away in defeat.

Later, I felt compelled to revisit my amends. Remember, I am a people pleaser by nature, and this episode was killing me on the inside. You should have seen their eyes and posture as I once again approached their cabana.

As the father began to stand, this time I asked if I could explain myself. I proceeded to tell them that I had suffered a devastating loss and was not myself. "Again, I just wanted to tell you how very sorry I am," I said.

One of the men in the group said, "So you don't want to fight me?" With that, we laughed a little. I cried a little. I healed, just a little.

That was a rough day. I had very little emotional strength. Now I was mad at God but also needed to forgive myself. I kept trying to journal. I wrote about it and often sarcastically asked God to somehow help me if He wasn't too busy with the other people He was allowing terrible and unfair things to happen to. I proceeded to tell God I was disappointed in how He was treating me. I demanded He show me some comfort. I would be needing miraculous signs and wonders to ease my weary soul. But mostly I just wanted God to tell me how sorry He was for taking Charley from me.

For a long time after Charley died, I felt like a spoiled teenager when talking to God, and frankly, I didn't care. I was always mad, with arms folded and feet stomping. I demanded answers, all the while craving his comfort. I journaled and yelled and threw all-out temper tantrums to exhibit my disdain at my current situation and God's poor decision-making. I wrote harsh words to God about it all.

Looking back, I am not surprised, but I am grateful that God "took it on the chin" from me. He didn't get mad at my seemingly ungrateful attitude or use of foul language. I cussed like a sailor at Jesus, and He still loved me. Because it's our relationship that matters. Ours was built on trust from the past many decades, not on these present-day harsh words or hurt feelings. He understood my pain because He went before me in it. He loved me right where I was in those moments. I needed that. We all do.

Psalm 73:26 (NIV) says: *My flesh and my heart may fail, but God is the strength of my heart and my portion forever.*

Triggers and Stressors

I asked myself, what was the *why* behind my behavior at the water park? There is always a reason. I am a firm believer in identifying the why, so I can learn and grow. To find the why, we must be willing to look a little deeper. It came to me as I journaled.

It's similar to a wife yelling at her husband for not drying the dishes correctly. She may or may not care about the dishes, but she does care that they haven't talked or been affectionate for three months, and she feels unheard and unseen. You get the picture. In grief, it is often not about the dishes.

A year earlier, Charley and I had put off a lot of things due to COVID, including our marriage. In July 2021, we decided we weren't going to put things off any longer and snuck away for a little trip to the Caribbean to a small, secluded island off St. Thomas. It was wonderful. We barely talked to anyone else, and we went to a small beach called Honeymoon Beach. I remember thinking I'd like to come back when we got married. We spent several days there doing mostly nothing but swimming with the sea turtles in the lagoon and sitting under **our cabana**.

There it was! The cabana had triggered me without me even realizing it. I now knew *why* I had acted in such an uncharacteristic way. It wasn't planned or intentional, and now I knew that it wasn't really about the cabana. It was Charley. It was grief.

I had been irrational and even mean on that occasion, but it was easier for me to forgive myself once I realized the underlying issue. This insight also helped me to journal and talk about it with safe friends. I knew now I was grieving the thought of what could never be. A dream where we married and went back to our island, our cabana, our future.

I needed to process this trigger. I had to face head-on the realization that Charley had no future and mine no longer included him. I needed to understand this type of stressor and use calming tools to deal with it in order to cope better. These tools would ultimately help me to be more aware of my triggers before I had a *next time*.

One of the most important lessons I've learned through my own pain is this: When people exhibit bad behavior, instead of immediately asking, "What's wrong with them?" it is more helpful and certainly more compassionate to ask, "What happened to them?"

Hurt people hurt people. I'm people. You're people. We hurt.

A few weeks after cabana-gate, I went to the chiropractor in an attempt to put into practice some deeply needed self-care. I was continuing to struggle to regulate my emotions. I was continuing to journal and this entry reminds me of the slow, but continual progress I was making.

> Had a very emotional morning. Cried a lot and wanted to stay in bed. I decided to take some opposite action to combat my feelings of sadness, so I went to the chiropractor. I was lying on the table and in walks Seth, my friend of many years and the pastor who officiated at Charley's funeral. I had some overwhelming feelings as soon as I saw his face. It was like Charley was there in that office somehow, and I jumped off the chiropractor's table to hug Seth as if he were Charley in the flesh. It was weird, but I really needed that hug.

After reflecting, I realized that it may have been more of an *attack* than a hug. It was impulsive and a bit erratic. I messaged Seth that evening and explained that I had had a *morning of mourning* and apologized for "attacking him." He, of course, said, "A hug from you is never an attack."

Later as I was telling my daughter about the day and the attack on Seth, she reminded me that I was a work in progress. "Good progress, Mom," she said. "At least you didn't assault any innocent families on vacation today."

Emotions and feelings can be our friends or our enemies; we usually get to choose, but not always. I chose early on to accept being angry and irritated as part of my grief, keeping in mind that it wasn't permanent. Grief can make us feel completely out of control. If we choose to act like it's not an issue and take no action, emotions and feelings can rule us. We can get increasingly bitter instead of better. Emotions run high during grief, and we need to express them in safe ways, with safe people.

We must talk our pain to death.

Negative feelings will show up alive and well later if we are not active in accepting them as part of the current grief process. Charley would say, "You must talk your emotions and feelings to death, or you'll try and bury them alive." I will go one step further and say if you don't bury those emotions dead, they can easily come back to life when you least expect it. Like at a water park?!

I want to give you a challenge as we wrap up this chapter. Begin a journal. Before you throw a hard no, hear me out. It's okay if you don't journal. It can feel difficult, but remember, feelings are unreliable. Give it a try for a few days and see if it helps. If you hate it, it's cool. Try again another time.

Either way, offer yourself and others grace around the mix of emotions today. Grief makes me think of Forrest Gump's mom when she said, "Life is like a box of chocolate, you never know what you're gonna get." When you feel your heartbeat rise or your emotions flare uncontrollably, don't lose sight of the truth. You are an average human, doing the best you can today. And if you lose your cool, think about it; the why. Maybe journal, and you may just find out it's not really about the dishes.

CHAPTER 3
DON'T JUDGE

Before you judge me make sure you're perfect.
— Ziad K. Abdeinour

One theme you will hear me reference repeatedly is the warning about being judgmental. This means of others and, even more importantly, of yourself. There is no handbook for how we feel, act, or respond when bad things happen. You will grieve how you grieve; someone else will do it completely differently. Don't judge.

It had been a couple of months since *it* happened. It was quiet now, and I was alone more. From the moment this tragedy happened, family and friends had been by my side. My kids stayed with me and handed me off like a relay-race baton. So many friends took turns *babysitting* me. (That's what I called it because I felt unable to care for myself at times.) Loved ones helping me get through one terrible day after the next. But people have to return to their lives and routines and I, somehow had to find a new way with a new me.

Alone isn't a fun place to be when grief is fresh. I had to start figuring out how to make it through time and space again without someone always holding my hand. Without *him* holding my hand.

Your loss may be a person you spent every day with, maybe not. Whatever circumstances you face, learning to cope in this new atmosphere becomes tricky.

It may seem impossible in the beginning. You know what else seemed impossible for me in the first couple of months after Charley died? Everything.

Simple things, regular things, new things, all things. Everything felt like work, and I didn't have the energy to do work. Sometimes just breathing felt like work. I had to get very black and white to progress in the early days of my grief. I would try to pump myself up, encourage myself. I'd say things like, "How about brushing your teeth, Julie? You can do that today, right?" I talked to myself a lot and tried to remember how Charley would say things to me like, "You better talk nice to the woman of my dreams." How freaking adorable is that! I really wanted to take everyone's words to heart and be kind to myself, but that proved difficult early on.

Getting out of bed and brushing your teeth each day sounds simple. Remember, as we progress, many things sound simple. Simple, yes. Easy, no. Still, to this day, I remind myself of this often to keep my expectations in line. Even things that were once simple now feel hard.

When loss is fresh, everything you do reminds you of your person and what happened. Conversely, anything that isn't about them, frankly, you don't really give a hoot about it. This loss is big, huge. It's all-consuming and impossible for anyone who isn't you to grasp the gravity of the consumption. So, let's brush our teeth.

I went into the bathroom. I grabbed my electric cleaning machine, started to brush, and immediately started to cry. As I stood with this vibrating brush in hand, weeping for what would appear to anyone else to be for no good reason, I recalled why I was standing at the "not so tall" sink.

My vanity had two sinks: one "tall" and one "not so tall." I'm five foot nine inches, so I had always used the "tall" sink. After Charley's proposal, I decided I would need to get used to using the "not so tall" sink. After all, my fiancé was six foot five inches, so this made sense. The thought of sharing was both nerve-wracking and exciting to think about.

I gave Charley an electric toothbrush like mine (his and hers toothbrushes, super romantic) and plugged it in at the "tall sink" side. I even started sharing by emptying one drawer for him to put a few things in on the occasions when he would need them prior to our nuptials.

Now as I stood there looking in the mirror brushing my teeth, the tears and the reality hit simultaneously, that he is never going to use any sink. Tall, not so tall, who even cared? He is not coming back. I slumped down flat on the floor like a lifeless ragdoll, spit running out of my mouth, the salty tears mixing with the mint-flavored paste.

This was the reality of getting through the simplest of tasks. In the beginning, I barely did. Everyone is different. We have to take things slow and move with the ebb and flow of how our body and mind direct and allow us. I didn't seem to be fully in charge of my emotions, so I had to surrender to whatever came next and not judge.

All or Nothing

On any given day I felt every emotion or no emotions at all. I had many days and moments resembling the bathroom incident. Everything from looking at meat in Costco (the same meat he would meticulously pick out to cook for our Easter dinner) or the grocery store where I was accustomed to buying "my brand" and "his brand" of water. I automatically grabbed for *his* water and quickly came to the realization he didn't need water. Not today, not ever. I would experience a day of uncontrollable emotions and then, with no warning, the following day I would wake up and feel, well, nothing.

Everyone expects to feel sadness with grief, even anger and such, but did you know that feeling numb is also a very common feeling after loss?

Being numb, as long as it is not chemically induced, is not wrong. I believe it is especially important not to judge on this kind of day. Grief will attempt to shame you if you allow it.

In the beginning of the grieving process, I felt numb at different times. My numbness set in during the funeral and throughout some of the busyness of handling all the unwanted tasks that need to be done after your person dies. Sometimes I felt numb on a random day, for no apparent reason. Feeling numb is not being cold, unfeeling, or even, dare I say, strong. You are still smack dab in the middle of grieving.

Frankly, I began to pray for numbness. I welcomed it in a big way because I felt like I could breathe easier on those days. In extreme trauma, I believe numbness is one of the tools God gives us to cope. Scientifically speaking, feeling emotionally numb commonly arises as an unconscious protective response to feeling difficult emotions. We can feel this way in a variety of emotional states, including but not limited to anxiety, stress, or trauma. Experts at the National Library of Medicine[1] regard emotional numbness as a form of dissociation also called "emotional blunting." It can be useful as it allows us to unconsciously protect ourselves from extreme emotional pain, as long as this does not become a persistent or permanent state of emotional being.

Some days, our brains just need a break.

Of course, we don't want numbness to be the only emotion we feel or go on for extended periods of time. We will feel all the different feels through the process of grief. We must sit in all of the pain, but at times numbness can be a welcomed relief in this ongoing and unwanted rollercoaster.

It's Okay to be Okay

You may hear that "it's okay that you're not okay." I get that, and I totally agree. But what about when we have those moments, days, and eventually longer periods of time when we actually start feeling okay?

The first time I experienced some feelings of being *okay* after Charley died was a few months after his death. I was in a place with a safe and loving community. They also missed him. Suddenly, I felt some relief and even found myself smiling and having some new conversations with people. Conversations that were not about *it*.

This caught me off guard, and I quickly realized I had forgotten about my pain, just for a minute. It felt weird at first, even, dare I say, wrong? People were talking and bustling about. The world was revolving, and I was still a part of it. It felt surreal. I watched and pondered my own feelings.

I wanted to talk to someone about this, and I was blessed to have a trusted friend nearby named Darrell. He was a dear friend of Charley's and had tragically lost his son Drew two years prior, so I knew he was ahead of me on the journey and would understand without judging me. I told him I was feeling strangely *okay* at that moment, and it felt weird.

He kind of chuckled and said, "Enjoy this, Julie. It's okay to be okay." Darrell went on to say, "Don't let anyone tell you differently, because tomorrow could be very different."

His words were true and wise. It continues to be a roller coaster, but I became very aware that on those beautiful days, those moments that offered some relief, that I needed to be intentional about allowing it to be okay. No shame allowed.

Harper Lee, in *To Kill a Mockingbird,* said it perfectly, "You never really understand a person until you consider things from his point of view; Until you climb inside of his skin and walk around in it."

Oh, that we could actually put ourselves in another's skin for even a moment. What a difference it would make. We truly would cease being so judgmental of others because we would be able to clearly understand them. We might even accept them right where they are. When we don't understand, we tend to judge. Yes, you; yes, me. We judge ourselves, and we judge others. It's human nature.

If you don't understand it, how can you possibly judge it?

When I'm thinking of judgment, my mind always goes straight to Jesus in John 8:1-11 where a woman was about to be stoned for her transgressions. This story of His great compassion brings me to tears regularly. Not only did He exhibit great compassion but also wisdom.

Jesus knew they were trying to trap Him in a religious debate. This woman had done things, yes (like you and me), but Jesus pointed out that if someone, anyone in the crowd was sinless, they should feel free to throw the first stone. He was kind and also truthful. He loved her and told her to "go and sin no more." Both truth and grace are possible at the same time.

In my grief, I immediately became more judgy of myself and others. In the early days and months, judgment somehow became a go-to reaction for me. It felt somehow like I had the "right" to behave badly in my pain, and I often justified this due to my feelings of abandonment by God and Charley. Feelings are always real, often valid, but mostly unreliable.

Let's not judge ourselves too harshly. The less we do, the more that posture will filter out to others. It frankly can feel impossible to come to terms with all these ginormous emotions. How can we accept these drastic ups, downs, and all arounds? It's no easy task. Grief is living and breathing. We can't work it away, drink it away, or use any other *thing* or *one* to make it cease. Greif will wait for you to finish; it's patient.

I knew people wanted to say the right things to me in my pain. I knew they might be nervous or not truly think about what their words might mean to someone in a grief state. But platitudes and little pithy comments can unintentionally hurt.

I grew weary of statements about how Charley earned his angel wings. I would think to myself, "That statement for sure isn't biblical, and Charley wasn't an angel on earth. I don't think he will be in heaven either." I felt snarky thinking that, but the thought of this big burly man I loved with angel wings was not helpful as I continued to internally scream "Why God?!" over and over. My deep pain brought forth an internal judgmental response fairly often.

Another and very common painful comment no one in the grasp of great pain needs to hear is "Everything happens for a reason." I would think, "If you say that to me, you better have *said reason* and tell me ASAP, cause I'm all ears."

My advice for those who don't know what to say is to simply say, "I'm so sorry, and I don't know what else to say." Unfortunately, sometimes during grief and loss, well-meaning comments coming from well-meaning people, can sound well... mean.

I am certain I have said similar things to people and likely caused harm during their deepest grief. We don't know what we don't know. My hope is that talking about this openly will help us do better.

On the other side of the coin, I had a great appreciation for people being blunt and *not* acting like the loss didn't happen or it wasn't that bad. Maybe we don't always know what to say, but at the very least, be real and always speak that person's name. This alone can be so healing. A simple sentence like, "This sucks; it's terrible. I'm so sorry to hear about Charley." Thank you for saying his name.

Sharing a nice memory or saying they are missed is so refreshing and always welcome.

Simple statements and reminders that they are not forgotten are like a soothing salve to the soul of one whose heart is still freshly damaged.

Comfort comes in many ways. We can get it from God, our families, and others, but the reality is, we will eventually need to find ways to self-soothe.

Self-soothing comes more naturally to some than others. Regulating emotions takes practice. Emotions are tricky little buggers. They come and go as they please and show up uninvited on a regular basis like an unwelcome uncle at Christmas. The concept of self-soothing is important to address and, as I have learned over the years, can also be referred to as regulating or grounding.

Grounding

After Charley passed away, I was blessed to be given some time away from work. What to do with said time was the real question. I absolutely did not want to go to work or do my usual day-to-day operations. I just couldn't imagine it. But how do we alleviate some of this pain when we have time to kill? I didn't feel like doing anything!

I tried all kinds of things to help myself in the early days of my grief. Stay busy. Stay asleep. Eat massive amounts of ice cream. Watch countless hours of mindless shows on Netflix. Exercise excessively. How do we pass the time and cope with devastating loss without turning to negative thoughts and behaviors?

One of the healthier ways I have been attempting to do this is to use a technique called grounding. According to the University of New Hampshire's Physiological Counseling Services[2]: "Grounding is a self-soothing skill to use when you are having a bad day or dealing with a lot of stress, overwhelming feelings, and/or intense anxiety. Grounding is a technique that helps keep you in the present and helps reorient you to the here-and-now and to reality."

Grounding has been my way of relocating my "center." Coming back to the present.

I think of the past; I mourn the lost future. Both of these places are negative to my healing. The past keeps me stuck in a depressive state of regret, and worrying about the future causes me anxiety. I must find ways to return to the present to have a more peaceful mind.

There are many ways and versions of how to apply this broad term of grounding. One example is the 5 4 3 2 1 grounding technique. This technique asks you to find five things you can see, four things you can touch, three things you can hear, two things you can smell, and one thing you can taste. It doesn't have to be in that specific order. For example: I see five windows; I can touch a desk, a chair, a computer, a phone, and so on. We use our senses to distract our thoughts. Your brain has no choice but to focus on what is being asked of it. This welcomed distraction brings us back to the here and now, at least for a moment.

I used this technique early on to bring myself back to a calmer state when I would have what felt like a hundred-foot wave repeatedly trying to drown me. The concept is taking your mind somewhere else, anywhere else, away from what is causing the negative emotions. Even using a quick version of grounding, such as holding onto ice cubes for sixty seconds proves to be a fast and reliable way to temporarily bring back a place of calm.

Another effective way to ground yourself is intentional breathing. Listening to your breath, breathing deeply, holding your breath, and then taking a long exhale. One technique you can look up is "Box Breathing."

Search "grounding" online, and you will find endless ways to do it. But for me, I wanted to find things that helped me have longer periods of time where I could be grounded.

Full transparency: Food and TV were my go-to's in the beginning and can still be at times. That's okay, but we don't want to stay in unhealthy habits for long. My pain was so severe in the early months that I yearned for relief however I could find it. I picked some of the lesser evils for me, which were TV and food. As I felt the desire to do better, I looked for healthier ways.

One of the ways was doing puzzles. Another way was coloring. It is absolutely healthy for adults to do things that brought us joy as children. I highly recommend going back to things you loved as a child and trying them again. I have come to love coloring again, even though I'm not great at it. I love finding the best markers, books, etc. It has been fun. I will always recommend fun as a companion to mourning.

In the earlier months of grieving, activities like puzzles took up bigger chunks of time, in a good way. Chunks of time I would need filled now. I didn't want to sit alone, endlessly crying, or find myself in a pity party during the empty hours. As long as I concentrated on what was in front of me, it was easier not to focus purely on my sadness.

Nature and walking or hiking are other ways I found relief, and I have continued to use them on a regular basis to ground myself.

Activities that provide a healthy mind distraction. This is grounding in a nutshell. You will need to find what activities work for you.

Start small and find something that removes you from the heaviness of the moment, something that allows you to recenter and regulate your thoughts and emotions. And, above all, if it's hard or you don't get relief as quickly as you had hoped for, remember; don't judge. You are a work in progress, and you are doing the best you can with what you have today.

As you search for comfort, take things as slowly or as quickly as you are able. We are all so very different. Some will find healing in getting right back at it; some won't; some can't. Some of us will have more "time off" or away from work and the typical day-to-day stuff. Some will get thrown right back in. In the US, we are unfortunately not legally required to be paid for any time of grieving. Many countries now have laws in place for a couple of days with pay, but that is obviously still not enough. We humans are so focused on success and "doing" that we can miss the importance of healthy healing by not understanding how hard it is to grieve.

Using your words will be hard but important in the early part of your healing. No one can read your mind. Ask for what you want and need. You may or may not get it, but go ahead and ask. If you need time off, ask for it. If you need time alone, ask for it. If you don't get it, you will have to decide what your next steps are.

If you can't afford time off, that is so very hard, and I'm so very sorry. Continue to find ways to love yourself. Go for a walk during your lunch break. Don't pretend everything is okay. Step away when needed; speak your truth; cry in the bathroom; I've done this quite often. Be as vulnerable as you're able with safe people. Identify some grounding techniques and put them into practice.

As you return to work and public life, you may feel that no one understands, and you will be correct, most don't. Let yourself off the hook today and try some grounding. Find your center.

A dear friend sent me a song shortly after Charley died, and it impacted me greatly, as music often does. Music is a powerful grounding technique. The song, "A Reminder" by Trevor Hall, was a good grounding song for me. Find your place and what works for you. Don't compare yourself to anyone else.

In Scripture, God cautions us not to compare, because as we discussed earlier, unless we get the chance to literally walk in their skin, no one can truly understand what another is going through. "But when they measure themselves by one another and compare themselves with one another, they are without understanding" (2 Corinthians 10:12, ESV). Compare leads to despair, and if there is one thing we don't need more of, it's despair.

Comparison ultimately leads us to judgment of ourselves and others. Lyanla Vanzant said: "Comparison is an act of violence against oneself." You are loved right where you are today. Jesus reminded us over and over, in so many words, *just love*, this includes yourself.

---

1. "Inpatients experiences about the impact of traumatic stress on eating behaviors: an exploratory focus group study," *National Library of Medicine*, (2021) https://www.ncbi.nlm.nih.gov/pmc/articles/PMC8474934/
2. *What Is Grounding.* University of New Hampshire, Psychological and Counseling Services, 2024. https://www.unh.edu/pacs/what-grounding

CHAPTER 4
GRIEF TRAPS

A trap is only a trap if you don't know about it.
If you know about it, it's a challenge.
— China Mieville

 f we use the word *should*, it's important we are one hundred percent certain we are delivering true and accurate information. There are only a few specific times I feel the word *should* is appropriate. For example, if it's a life-threatening or dangerous situation, I may say, "You should be careful" or "You should stop doing that." If you are behaving in a manner that is truly harming someone else, I would be bold and tell you, "You should stop that" I would possibly *should* on *you* in those contexts.

I will not presume to know what someone should do or what someone needs. Even if I believe I have a good idea or that my experience may be helpful, I will *ask* if they would like me to share. After all, I'm not in their skin and can't know for sure, so why not ask?

After Charley died, I was told the following statement by someone who truly cares about me: "You *should* be happy he is in heaven and out of pain." Should I?

I was also told, "God must have needed Charley; that *should* make you feel some relief." That's gonna be a hard no from me. God doesn't *need* any of us and didn't need Charley, but I did.

Refrain from telling others how they *should* be feeling. There are some additional and equally hurtful phrases that are unproductive and can be considered hurtful and/or negative grief traps.

Grief traps sneak into our minds when we are weak. They have a way of knowing we may be temporarily defenseless, so they strike while the iron is hot.

As I started processing what took place after Charley died, I fell into one of the worst and most common traps. I started immediately spiraling into the *doubt and regret* traps. I began looking back and beating up on myself and sometimes on Charley. I started obsessing about all the things I could now do nothing about. My flesh and my unwelcome inner critic began saying stupid, pesky trap statements like,

- You should have…
- If only I (he) had …
- What if I (he) would have …
- Could have, would have, should have.
- Shame, blame, doubt, regret.

It's all a trap.

If your trap statements are surfacing while reading this, stop right here. Breathe. In for four, hold for four, out for four. Good job.

Those statements are all traps. By definition, traps are set intentionally and meant to hurt us. There are a lot of reasons why tragedy happens, but most of the time what happens is not our fault, and frankly, we're not powerful enough to have changed it. I say this in pure love, in hopes of giving us all some true perspective. Release yourself of the pressure, because you and me, we are not God.

If you would have had the power to save them, you would have. I believe you.

We are human, so it is natural for the regrets to start surfacing in a traumatic situation. It's also true that it tends to happen immediately. For me, my mind and emotions go there like clockwork. The what ifs and if onlys? Traps! The tidal wave of unwanted questions infiltrates my wounded mind on repeat.

The big one for me over the years has been, "Did they know how much I loved them?" With Charley, there were more and harder questions. Was he thinking of me? Did he suffer? Did I make him happy? Why didn't I marry him sooner?

Our brain feels like it will explode with these irrational ideas that have no solutions. No pills, condolences, or wisdom seem to make them stop. We must be committed to take action and stop these grief-traps in their tracks and quickly. This is where a practice of mindfulness comes in. The topic and word mindfulness is thrown around a lot today, so I will elaborate on what it means to me.

When I speak of mindfulness, I am referring to a therapeutic definition like this from Advizehealth[1]: "A mental state achieved by focusing on one's awareness on the present moment, while calmly acknowledging and accepting one's feelings, thoughts and bodily sensations."

Working on achieving a calmer mind takes just that, work. We must decide to think about what we are thinking about. Particularly during times of great grief, this can be a daunting task. In 2 Corinthians 10, God reminds us of this by suggesting we *take our thoughts captive*. I like this visual and think of it like this: I'll put those thoughts in jail and then immediately on trial. I am seeking truth and justice, so this makes sense. Once I make the determination that a thought may not be truthful, I am able to treat it more appropriately. I find that the majority of the time, these thoughts are one hundred percent false and they deserve the death penalty. They gotta go.

According to the Laboratory of Neuroimaging at the University of Southern California[2], the average human has about 70,000 thoughts a day. It makes me tired just thinking about that! Emotions and feelings give us thoughts. Thoughts lead to actions (good and bad), and over time, actions can lead us to habits. It's all connected, and it starts up in our noggin.

The brain is a magnificent organ but when used incorrectly, it can cause much harm. In addition to the struggle in our minds, there is an enemy who would love for us to lose all faith and hope after a trauma. God has a plan for each of us but let us not forget, so does our enemy. I may not completely understand God's plan, but I know I must practice healthy mindfulness to not only combat the enemy, but to combat my own weak flesh and, frankly, a sometimes grief-ignorant society. It's a big battle.

The world is a busy place, and there is so much competition for time with our brains. It can sometimes make it difficult to challenge our own thoughts. Instead, we may find ourselves agreeing with lies and irrational thoughts. We see social media, fake news and fluff that make us feel inferior. If we aren't careful, we start listening to others who may simply demonstrate a general lack of empathy for those struggling. Most humans do this unintentionally, but they still do it.

For me, and this is me being as vulnerable as it gets with you, the one statement that trapped me and was absolutely the most disturbing was, "Too bad you weren't already married, so he would have been living at your house."

I won't apologize for being upset about this. Some people actually say shit without thinking. It felt like a flaming, poisonous dart had entered my heart. Without thinking, a human who loves me drew back their bow and shot this arrow right into my soul.

Proof that words hurt, this statement prompted a very painful journal entry.

> *I'm so sorry I didn't hurry up and just get married to you, babe. How will you ever forgive me? I know it's not my fault, but it feels a little like it is. Why would God want us to end so soon? Did I make it happen because I had doubts? You knew right? You know how much I love you, right? You had to know. I pray you knew.*

This reality was difficult for me to swallow. I'm sure some of you can relate to this regret. For me, after a lot of anger, sadness, and reflection, I came to realize that this statement hurt so deeply because I had thought the same thing myself right after he died. No one needed to say it out loud. I was already thinking.

Escaping a Trap

I want to pause and revisit the definition of mindfulness: "A mental state achieved by focusing on one's awareness of the present moment, while calmly acknowledging and accepting one's feelings, thoughts and bodily sensations." As time put more distance between me and my loss, I didn't feel the sting of that hurtful statement as intensely. Distance for grief does help ease intensity, but reconciling this pain took work. Grief traps try to chip away at our serenity.

I took the time to analyze and find the truth about this topic. It looked something like this.

First, I needed to recognize the facts. Charley and I made an intentional choice to live separately until we were married. We had postponed the wedding during COVID and failed to set a new date. Waiting to live together until our marriage was a personal choice, and we *both* chose it. He's dead, and I feel like I'm here holding the bag. A bag full of choices I wish I could change but can't.

I suppose it makes sense that when I found out what happened to Charley, one of my first grief traps was feeling responsible for his death. Somehow, in my grief, shame, and regret, I decided that I was powerful enough to have saved him and had apparently made our relationship decisions all on my own. Therefore, I must carry some of the blame. I had to challenge this trap and fast. I had to take this thought and go to court.

> "Your honor, what exactly am I at fault for? Was I solely responsible for the decision that could have been a lifesaver, literally in his case?"

> "No, Julie, you made that decision together, and that decision did not cause Charley to die."

> "Did I cause the fire? Did I actually have any power or responsibility in this tragic accident?"

> "Of course not. No, Julie, you're not that powerful."

It was all a trap. It even sounds a little silly when I look back now, to think I could actually have changed the tragedy or stopped it from happening, but it didn't feel silly in the early moments of my grief.

Today I am fully aware I carry no responsibility for any of it. I didn't cause that terrible thing to happen. Nevertheless, feelings are real and persistent, even while remaining relentlessly unreliable! This blame was a lie, and this way of thinking is destructive. It's a grief trap.

There is a saying in Al-Anon, a recovery group for those supporting addicts, about taking undue responsibility for others' actions. It's referred to as the Three C's. "I didn't *cause* it. I can't *control* it. And I can't *cure* it."

For the loss of life, I take some liberty and change the last C to, I can't *change* it. It sucks, but this is the truth, and I have had to continue working on accepting this new reality in order to regain and maintain my peace.

> Whatever decisions you did or didn't make, they are done. It's over, and there is no going back. The truth is, we don't know if different decisions or choices would have changed the outcome.

The harsh reality is we will never know while we are here on earth. My suspicion is that if, and hopefully when, we get to heaven, it won't matter to us anyway. What we can do now is seek ways to stop the unhelpful hamster wheel in the head from spinning in our minds with its unproductive and damaging internal debate.

But what about the loss of a loved one you believe could have been prevented? Tragedy happens every day, and sometimes it's simply a terrible and innocent accident. When it's an accident or disease, including mental health and addiction, that's where we must leave it.

In addiction and mental health, I've witnessed the blame trap. Addicts and those with mental illness are often blamed for their own deaths. "They were so selfish!" "Why didn't they just stop?" From my own experience, during my darkest times of addiction and mental health struggles, I truly never wanted to hurt myself or anyone else. It was not something I intentionally set out to do. But I wasn't able to *just stop*. The "Just Say No" campaign of the 1990s failed for a reason, it's not realistic with illness. I was sick. So were they.

I hope you can allow that statement to help you heal if that is your loss situation. Please don't allow the grief trap of blame to halt your process of healing.

Many hurt people go straight to blame because they need an outlet for the pain. This happens all too often in accidental death as well. I understand feeling it, the blame, but I don't recommend it. I'm not saying there are no valid causes for lawsuits, etc. What I am talking about is the condition of your heart during these trials.

I can hear Charley saying to me still, "How's your heart?"

Accountability and consequences are part of life, but you can hold someone accountable while still showing compassion. What a gift to yourself and them. Remind yourself it was an accident and "But for the grace of God, there go I." Steer clear of assigning either blame or shame.

After Charley died, my kids and I went as a family to visit his roommate, John, right away. He had narrowly made it out of the fire with his life. I did not want him to have any guilt for surviving. Survivor guilt is real, and I would never wish that on anyone.

John had also lost everything, including his best friend. I was so grateful he had made it out, and I wanted to tell him those words in person. I loved him; so did Charley. He needed to hear that. There were no questions about the how and why on that day. No blame, no shame. Just simply sorrow and sadness.

What good could anything else have done to this already terrible, accidental situation? Not everyone's situation is the same. But erring on the side of kindness will save you heartache in the future.

I'll never forget my son's response after we left John that day. He looked at me and said, "Mom, I wasn't sure it was a good thing to go there to see him so soon. I thought it might be too hard. Now I see it was the beginning of the healing. What a life lesson in love you taught me today."

I spoke to John many times after that, and we did some healing together. Unfortunately, John died not long after Charley. The decision to love won again. People in pain don't need more pain. *If you can't be supportive, stay away until you can be.*

Death happens in many ways, and situations are all unique. I also want to address loss and death when caused intentionally. It's like grief on steroids. I know this terrible agony all too well. I first experienced it with the murder of my grandmother (which I talk about in chapter 6) and later in one of the most horrific murders in the history of Indianapolis.

My dear friend Magno and six more of his family members, including three children, were murdered in a senseless robbery. To this day, it remains difficult for my brain to really grasp.

When it came time to sentence the two men who had committed the crimes, Magno's wife, Kim, called and informed me that she and Magno's daughter, Jasmine, would *not* be asking for the death penalty.

When I asked how and why she was able to forgive the two men, she said, "I couldn't hate them for what they did and still raise my daughter to love. If I carry the hate, so will she, and I am determined not to let that happen."

She continued, "The only way I've made it is God. I have no other way to explain, because there were days I thought there was no way I could continue, and yet I did."

It's a heart condition. Nothing about this makes sense. Notice she said there were days she didn't think she'd make it. That reality is part of our grief journey. Kim went on to tragically lose another husband, but I am continually encouraged by my friend who is now happily remarried and is a grandmother of two. Others' stories remind us that we can and will get through this.

About my grandmother's murder, I had a lot of mixed feelings later in life when I learned the men who killed my grandmother were two young men, addicts. I had to work through that, once again pondering the statement, "But for the grace of God, there go I." I had to humble myself and consider the difficult question: Is it possible that at the height of my own addiction I could have found myself in a disastrous situation with disastrous outcomes?

I'm not saying I would be capable of such a heinous crime, but as I worked an inventory (Step 4 in a 12-step recovery) of my emotions surrounding this painful loss, I talked to people I trusted. I practiced putting my thoughts on trial. In this way, I was able to see the criminal's brokenness alongside my own shortcomings and frailty. I was able to move forward from some of the anger and blame I had been trapped in. I even felt some sadness and compassion for them and began to wonder, not so much "How could you do that?" but "What happened to you?" I forgave them, and I felt more peace. It was for me, not them.

Sometimes our actions directly contribute to or even cause damage or death accidentally. If that's you, I want you to address this unique pain. Others may have done a lot of *shoulding* on you. You are likely *shoulding* on yourself as well. You are not what you did or what happened to you.

You are who you are today. At this very moment, you have a chance to start moving toward peace.

I've seen miraculous healing in this area over the years. No matter what your past looks like, without exception, there can be time and grace for you to heal. I don't know your specific situation, but if you can accept your part and find forgiveness for yourself, you can begin a healing journey.

If you did cause harm, it will likely start with you asking for and giving forgiveness to those involved, including yourself. First John 1:9 (NIV) is very clear on this topic: "If we confess our sins, he is faithful and just and will forgive our sins and purify us from all unrighteousness." If someone cannot or will not accept your apology, that is between them and God. You did your part. Now, go and sin no more.

You are never too far gone. God loves you, I love you, but there is work to do.

The Power of Community

Establishing the truth is crucial. Grief can be a liar. When we find ourselves spiraling emotionally and mentally, our community becomes vital. Who we spend our time with and what they believe is so important in times of great emotional exposure. When shame and regret tried to replace my better judgment, I went directly to people who knew me. Really knew me. Close friends and family who I trusted. People who I could tell honestly what I was thinking and could help me define it as truth or lie. If it was a lie, they would help me put it on trial and send it where it belonged.

Most of these thoughts were mental garbage that I needed to throw out. It's what I call *stinkin' thinkin'*. It really does stink, and we don't want it lingering in our clean space.

The unfortunate thing about how we think of ourselves is that according to The National Science Foundation[3], eighty percent of our 70,000 thoughts a day are negative and ninety-five percent of them are repetitive. Geesh. Repetitive, negative, and about ourselves.

I suggest asking friends and family you trust the same questions that are popping up in your head. I did this often, without warning, and at all hours of the day and night. I expressed some, mostly unwarranted, concerns that plagued my psyche like, "Did he know how much I loved him?" I would ask over and over in a spell of uncontrollable tears. I received the same answer over and over, "Absolutely, he did. And he loved you, Julie."

I may have worn out some of my people, some of his people, but that reassurance was what I needed to survive those dark episodes. I couldn't get it from him, so I had to find it elsewhere. I had to find comfort in my community, often and repetitively.

Repetition is important. When I was young, my dad used to tell me "practice makes perfect." That statement never served me well. It led me to believe that this was my father's expectation of me, to in fact be perfect. Since this was unrealistic, I began to overachieve and feel worthless with failures of nonperfection, believing I was not good enough.

Beliefs lead to actions and those actions often become habits. If they are negative beliefs, the habits we form from those lies can be destructive.

As an adult in recovery, I chose to change the statement to read like this: "practice makes progress." I like it so much better.

Hearing others I trust affirm and confirm truthful answers, repetitively, was so comforting to me in the early stage of my loss. I practiced asking the questions openly and often when I was struggling with doubt, and then I would try to focus on receiving the truth. Keep asking until you make enough progress to believe the truth for yourself. Practice makes progress, and progress breeds healing.

From the view of *someone loving someone who is hurting*, the topic of truth expands. When a person you love is grieving, we attempt to speak positive, loving encouragement whenever possible. "Truth in love" is important but stay away from being brutally honest. There is a big difference. While someone is grieving, they don't need any harsh truths or opinions. Keep any negativity you may have about the deceased (or the living) to yourself. There will be other times for different conversations.

At the early stage, attempt to support without judgment. Muster as much love and compassion as you are able in answering those sometimes irrational and repetitive questions. Even if it seems redundant, answer with kindness. It takes practice to believe a different reality. In these moments, you may even find you are uniquely positioned to give this person a little touch of comfort. Do it until you're sick of doing it, and then do it a few more times. You will never regret having been kind and patient to the ones you love.

> Everything about grief is hard, but we have tools to escape some of these hard places. If you find you are *shoulding* on yourself or someone else, try the practice of thinking about what you're thinking about today.

Let's get practical.

Write it down: What's trapping you? Blame? Regret? Find a person you trust and set up a time to talk to them and tell them the grief trap you are in. Allow them to help you identify what is true and what is false.

Take it to trial.
Take it to a friend.
Take it to the Lord.

It's important to have someone emotionally objective and kind. Ask your trusted one to remind you of these truths on a regular basis, to hold you accountable for being kind to yourself today. This does not all happen in one day. Processes take time and remember, dear ones, there is no time limit or deadline to impose on your healing.

Let's take a breath, a break, and a little inventory of how we are feeling. When I feel drained, it's a good signal that I need to focus on some mindfulness. When I read or write hard words, it can be exhausting. We need to protect our minds so we don't stay stuck in the yuck. I want to encourage you to pick a grounding exercise and give yourself some one-on-one time.

My mindfulness includes doing one single activity and not multitask-ing. I'll repeat, one thing at a time. This is actually difficult for me. If I need what I call "a checkup from the neck up," it's important to get a singular focus. This may look like watching a show I like but doing nothing else. No phone game, no folding laundry. Just listening and watching the story. The key here is to be fully present in whatever you are doing. One minded. Centered. Give it a try. You may be surprised how difficult that singular focus can be.

You are doing amazing things.
I am so very proud of you.
Now I'm gonna go start a puzzle.

---

1. *The Power of Mindfulness at Work*. Advize, (2020). https://advizehealth.com/the-power-of-mindfulness-at-work/
2. *Human Brain Shape Has Hardly Changed*. Evolution News, (2022). https://evolution news.org/2022/08/human-brain-shape-has-hardly-changed/
3. *Bothered by Negative, Unwanted Thoughts? Just Throw Them Away.* U.S. National Science Foundation, (2012).https://www.nsf.gov/news/news_summ.jsp?cntn_id=126164

CHAPTER 5
STRONG IS OVERRATED

But they who wait for the LORD shall renew their strength; they shall mount up with wings like eagles; they shall run and not be weary; they shall walk and not faint.
— Isaiah 41:31 (ESV)

*D*epending on the day and my emotions, when people say, "You're one of the strongest people I've ever known" can make me feel like a weakling. I know they mean well, but I don't want to feel as if I have to keep it all together all the time. The next sentence is very important for us all to understand.

In Grief, It is Important Not to Tell Someone How *They* Feel

Saying to me "You're so strong" implies that someone believes they know how I feel, and worse, that they have an expectation for me to uphold. When people say words like, "You're so strong" or "I can't believe how well you're holding up in this," they absolutely mean to compliment you.

But I'm letting you and me off the hook here and now. We do not have to be strong every day or any day, and we certainly do not need to act like we are okay when we are struggling with grief. Remember the saying, "It's okay, to not be okay"? It really is. Putting pressure on ourselves based on what we think others want is very unproductive. The likelihood is that you are already in pain or will find yourself in a grief situation at some point in the future. When that happens, I vow to never tell you how strong you are.

In the first couple months after Charley died, people were saying that phrase to me often. When I went back to work, hearing it I often felt somehow responsible for making others comfortable. My people pleasing reared its ugly head, and I had the desire to help *others* feel okay in *my* grief. This unrealistic expectation was self-inflicted, of course, but always hearing how strong I was didn't help my tired and hurting brain.

After a short cycle of people saying how great I was doing and me thanking them, all the while building resentment, I realized I was not going to be able to keep up that charade. In addition to that unrealistic public persona, I realized I wasn't going to be able to do my life the way I once had. I wasn't the same, not personally, and not at my job. It was all different. I was not able to function in the same capacity I once had.

My job was serving the public. Helping the hurting. It had been a joint effort. Charley and I had been a team, but now it was just me. They say there is no *I* in team, and they (whoever they are) are correct. For me to proceed at that level of care *alone* after such a tragedy, simply felt like too much.

It felt like too much because it was too much. I had to face the reality that I didn't want to do it anymore, not without him.

Maybe I did too much too soon. It was like me to cope by overworking. Maybe that season of my life was simply coming to an end. Whatever the reason, my mental and emotional self was not able to keep up with the demands, and so I decided to leave. I made the excruciating decision to leave a community and a career that I had built for almost twenty years. Grief changes everything.

I am in no way suggesting anyone quit doing anything. I am simply sharing my story and telling you a cautionary tale of pushing too hard, too soon. You get to decide how you feel and what you can and can't do after a traumatic loss. Well-meaning friends and family will do their best to guide and love you, but you are the only one who truly knows how strong or weak or hurt or able you are on any given day.

In our culture, there is a certain rush in the air. A rush for us to enter back into the norm and quickly. Go ahead and have your trauma-drama, and then we're gonna need you to get right back into the rat race. Sometimes when we are grieving, we have no idea what's good for ourselves. We are not of sound mind.

Unfortunately for me, I fell into the trap of "if they think I'm good, I must be good." This goes back to my very human condition and need for approval. I do not regret my decision to leave and believe it was what God wanted for me, but that didn't make it easy.

This being strong thing can be a real dilemma. We are capable people. Maybe you have those same overachieving characteristics in your life, maybe not. Whether you are type A, B, or XYZ, we all get to decide what is okay for us. I am fiercely independent, but in grief, that doesn't mean I feel strong. Let's try to understand the difference.

Someone appearing independent and showing up for responsibilities doesn't negate the fact that a person may actually feel terrible.

Looking and performing efficiently is not the same as feeling strong or peaceful inside. If someone appears to be doing okay, that's great. I would suggest you go ahead and ask them.

Asking questions is a good way to start a conversation when you don't know what to say. It's a lost art and a key component of good communication. Humans tend to want to fix and assume we have all the answers. It's not helpful to offer unsolicited opinions to others. What is helpful is asking how the person is actually feeling. "Are you feeling strong today?" It's a simple and important question and gives a chance for someone to answer honestly. It allows their voice to give an accurate accounting of their current strength and emotional level.

Ask someone who is grieving how they are feeling. Don't tell them by stating what you believe or hope is the answer.

Where did this strong thing come from, anyway? Perhaps it is a go-to comment because it's too hard and uncomfortable for others to see us grieve. Not everyone is great at condolences. Most are nervous or uncomfortable. And unfortunately, not everyone thinks a person needs very much time to grieve. Not everyone has grieved themselves, but at some point, it is inevitable. We all will. Anyone who loves someone will experience some type of grief. To love deeply is to grieve deeply. Trying to be strong for other people's benefit is exhausting, and we are already exhausted from grieving. Grieving is hard work.

Having said this, I don't want anyone to feel bad about things they have said or done in love. That is absolutely not my heart. I've done all the things I speak about on my own journey and now realize some were not helpful. I want us all to grow and heal together. I want to bring awareness to adjectives that feel bad to an already hurting person.

In loving those who are grieving, we must be intentionally slow to speak. The book of James is one of my favorites, and when I feel frustrated, I turn to it for guidance and truth. I don't always want to hear this truth, but I need it. The book of James is a truthful record about communication, recovery, and healing. In James 1:19 (ESV), he states, "Let every person be quick to hear, slow to speak, slow to anger, for the anger of man does not produce righteousness." Where was this reminder when I was at the water park?

We must consider and be sensitive to the way we communicate, especially with someone who is hurting. Think about your adjectives, they matter. I am grateful for books like James, even when it convicts me of my mistakes. I'm human, and I am certain some of my words have caused harm. As I feel and recognize how words have also stung me, I grow more and more passionate about learning, sharing, and getting better.

We're Just Not That Powerful

When people comment on how strong we are, they are usually talking about our physical and emotional strength. We appear well and upright, so we must be *fine*. We are smiling and interacting with the world without crying or appearing to be in a major depression, so we are obviously feeling back to our *old-self*. Most don't even realize that our *old-self* is gone and won't be coming back.

There is also a spiritual side of strength. Jesus spoke amazing words in his Sermon on the Mount, recorded in Matthew 5:5 (ESV) "Blessed are the meek, for they shall inherit the earth." Meekness is a big deal. Culture often implies that weakness is a direct result of acting meek. The two words are often used interchangeably, but I don't think this is accurate. I've witnessed the world act as if traits like compassion and even empathy equate to someone being fragile, or meek. I see culture assuming that meekness is someone not standing up for oneself or others. Or maybe someone not having the nerve to demonstrate some point of view, to be proven right or to possession something the world deems as *valuable*. I disagree and see meekness as a valuable and for me a coveted character trait.

When I feel *weak* on the other hand, I can resort to what I call *conditioning or my convincing mode*. I want everyone to agree with me. I'll state my evidence and show my frustration with conflicting points of view. If I can't get you to see my way, I may become easily offended and angry that I don't have the approval I desire to make me feel powerful. Whew. Meek and weak are different.

Jesus was the epitome of a meek man. He said those who are meek will inherit the earth. But why?

When I picture my Savior, I see the definition of meekness in real time. Gently, even submissive at times (I have never washed my friend's feet, maybe you have), but never weak. Not in the sense of seeking approval by using brash or disrespectful words to condition anyone into thinking a certain way. He is God. You get to choose to follow or not, based on His good examples. His meek examples.

The first time I discussed this topic was with Charley. The definition he shared with me was simple: *meek = strength under control.* That did it for me. This definition was everything. We can be strong but remain humble and vulnerable. We can be spiritually, physically, and emotionally strong while remaining soft hearted and kind.

Charley struggled with needing to always be *strong* due to his past abuse and trauma. Using strength as a self-protection tool had resulted in him causing harm to others, or as he would put it, "I learned to protect myself by making people cry with my words." This perceived strength may look tough on the outside; it may manifest itself as anger, sadness, or frustration, but in reality, it is simply a brick wall of self-protection. Charley told me early in our relationship about his desire to be meek and gentle despite the pain and loss he had experienced. He longed to exhibit the characteristics of Jesus, and meekness was first on his list.

I find it tragic the way a lot of men have been conditioned their whole lives to bury feelings and be the "tough guy." Guys are expected to be particularly strong and are often judged if they fail in this role. Our culture judges vulnerability and can assume it shows weakness of character, but that is clearly wrong. Strength under control is as manly as it gets. Jesus proved this over and over with his unmatched control and persistence of goodness, no matter how badly people treated him.

Being told I'm strong in grief produces the opposite feeling. It makes me feel exhausted, as if I should somehow have the answers or the abilities to easily cope with these unknown and terrible things. It feels like somehow, as an average human, I'm supposed to have power and knowledge that I can't possibly possess. Superhero kind of stuff, if you will.

Even superheroes have flaws and weaknesses.

I'm just lil' ole me, and I don't want to have to always *be* or worse yet, *act* a certain way for others. It's unrealistic and unhealthy. This too is a trap. A trap of pride.

Pride would tell us we've got this. Pride says I'm good and can do anything in my own strength and power. It eliminates the need for a Savior. "I can do all things through Julie, who gives me strength." Nope.

Spiritual strength is the opposite of this self-reliant thinking. Meekness reminds us that we can remain calm and serene in pain, yes, but also that we are not the ultimate source of strength. When we welcome meekness, we understand clearly that we are not the provider of strength. We can openly share our weaknesses and pain with others and with God without feeling shame, because alone, we are simply not that powerful. Charley always said, "I don't know how, but I know who." Simple and comforting.

No one should have to live up to the pressure of appearing invincible. How truly exhausting that would be. I want to understand my place in the universe and submit to the one who is truly in the ultimate strength position. Yeah, that would not be me.

I remind myself when working with others, that whether they do well or poorly, I don't get the credit. I am simply not that powerful. I can't take responsibility for someone else's wins or losses. Those are theirs. I am simply responsible for my own behavior and attitude. I continue to strive for my attitude and behavior to be influenced by turning my strength over to God.

No matter the circumstance, the apostle Paul reminds us in Philippians 4:13 (NKJV): "I can do all things through Christ who strengthens me."

A saying I heard early in my own recovery is "Self can't heal self."

Simply put, we cannot do this alone. We are not powerful enough to heal ourselves. We weren't designed that way. The mind is amazing, and I agree that healthy self-talk and mindfulness are vital. I've read and watched many studies that prove our thinking can be vital in the healing process, even in physical healing. It's fascinating and worth looking into, but our minds can only go so far.

When I refer to "self trying to heal self," I'm talking about self-reliance and an unwillingness to seek and receive help from others. I'm also talking about not allowing God to help in the process. In self-reliance, the world tends to get it backward. For example, with willpower. We see it in slogans like, "Just say no." or "Just do it." Go ahead and *will* yourself into a position of power, believing you need no one's help; but this is exhausting and tends to cause burn out or break down. There are certainly ways we can use our mind and wills to cope and heal that are not negative, but realistically and eternally, self needs help.

The book of Proverbs is a wise and honest account of good counsel from hundreds of years of experience and wisdom. To truly do some "self-help," read the book of Proverbs and apply it to your life.

Proverbs 3:5-6 (NIV) says it like this: "Lean not on your own under-standing; in all of your ways submit to him, and he will make your paths straight." This takes the pressure off me feeling the need to have all the answers.

Willpower to me today means something very different from when I was younger. Today, I ask God to *give me the power to accept his will in my life.* To accept that there are things I am and always will be completely powerless over. It's not a simple notion, but we all greatly need God to help us. We can allow God to remind us that we can't understand it all today, maybe ever. But as we struggle internally, we don't need to be alone. He will stay with us.

We don't need to *find the strength* to overcome this pain. In fact, with some help, maybe we can release this concept of willpower altogether, giving up the notion that we can *will ourselves into a position of strength.*

If the concept of God's love and help is hard for you today, maybe you can agree that, at the very least, we need each other.

Whatever your belief, if you can seek a power greater than yourself, if you can allow others in and lean on them when you're too weak, it can help with this road you're on. Those we turn to for additional support will remind us that it's not about mustering up or gritting our teeth. Grief is no time to "Suck it up, buttercup."

There have been many times that I couldn't pray. No words came, just groans or anger. In a state of rage and feeling betrayed, it occurred to me that God also hated death. So much so that He sent His Son to overcome it. I found comfort in this common hatred.

Early in my grief, I yelled and screamed and raged at God, but ulti-mately I realized that in doing these things, I was continuing to demonstrate my faith in Him. Was my faith shaken? Yes, but the mere fact that I was yelling at God indicated that I still believed He was there and listening to me. Even with all I said and felt about his fairness or lack of it, he remained present for me. In my weakest moments is where God shows up the strongest. Thankfully, I still believe His strength is sufficient in my weakness; more than sufficient.

As time progresses, I realize this "you're so strong" issue is mostly self-inflicted. No one ever actually told me that I *had* to be strong. That's my own demand placed on me by me. It goes back once again to that overachieving little girl and her desire to earn love and please those around her. I'm not her anymore. I don't have to be, and I choose not to be. You have also grown and changed. You're not the same child of your youth. You, too, can choose.

As I was researching the word *strong*, one definition from Websters I found was, "the ability to withstand great force or pressure." All I could think of was an old pressure cooker my dad had when I was a kid. It was made from some heavy metal, like an army tank, and had a lid that felt like it weighed about five pounds. In the pot you would put a big chunk of tough meat. Raw and tough. To make sure the pressure was sufficient, you fastened this helmet of a lid with screws until it was secure and you were fairly confident that under pressure the lid wouldn't pop off. Then you hoped that, due to the extreme pressure buildup, a couple hours later something would be pulled from this pressure abyss, steaming hot and miraculously tender.

This is how grief feels sometimes. Like I'm a raw piece of meat, and the pressure is getting to me. I don't want to live engulfed in the lie, telling me to have it all together in these pressure-cooker days of grief. I don't want my lid to pop off!

You know that saying "What doesn't kill you makes you stronger." Does it? I love me some Kelly Clarkson, but that's a hard no for me. Why must we glorify trauma? It is not something to be glorified! It sucks! It's not something we have been "blessed" with. Charley dying did not bless me! I am not stronger because of it. I am sadder. Can we use our lessons for good, for helping others? Yes, of course. But let's call a spade a spade. Trauma is dark, black, and pointy.

Trauma is not to be praised.

The truth about trauma is, if we don't seek help and safe people, it *can* in fact kill you. Studies have shown that trauma will attempt to dysregulate your nervous system. Left untreated, trauma may actually leave your nervous system in shambles, resulting in symptoms such as brain fog, chronic pain, hormonal imbalances, dizziness, digestive issues, and fatigue. These symptoms can lead us right down the anxiety and depression lane. It can be a vicious cycle if we ignore what trauma is doing to our bodies. Add in some extra, everyday stress and the list of disease and illness is endless. If you are experiencing extended, severe symptoms, I encourage you to seek medical or therapeutic help. At the very least, join a group of folks who are going through the same thing you are. People who truly understand.

One of the resources that has been healing for me is *Grief's Healing Choices*. This online group is designed to support people in their specific grief journey. I developed a circle of women who were experiencing the same loss that I was at the same time. That's the "me too" of community that is so healing.

My dear friend, Tina, who has a lot of unfortunate, first-hand knowledge of different types of trauma and loss, recently gave me these wise words. "Trauma has shaped me, yes. But made me stronger? Not so much. People see and want to believe you are strong, because they only see the surface, and it can make them feel more at ease. What they don't see is that you may be barely standing on shaky legs with an even shakier faith. They don't understand what it actually took for you to be in public. You didn't easily muster up the strength to be there. You knew you had to do it or let the grief and trauma hold you captive and watch you slip away and your life with it. Some days it's okay to just slip away, but we have to come to understand those boundaries so we don't get lost for good."

She went on to say, "When I'm hurting and people say 'God's gonna use this', I wanna smack em'. A love smack, of course. Some-one's standing there talking about how strong you are, and they have no clue how close you feel to being taken out of commission for good."

I got a good belly laugh out of the way she described the "love smack," and then she finished the conversation with this "mic-drop" moment. "It's probably going to take a lifetime of laughter to coun-terbalance the grief, but even still, the grief will always be there."

We aren't supposed to instinctively know how to deal with grief. This world is not how God originally planned it, so it would make sense that it isn't intuitive to deal with death and sorrow. Early in our grief journey, we tend to do a lot of acting to cover up our lack of understanding, but today I want to challenge us to end the charade. Resistance to emotional vulnerability can cause havoc. We may think, "I'm keeping this to myself to stay safe, or spare them my pain." Maybe you have trust issues (don't we all?), or you think, "They won't understand; it's too painful, and I have to be strong for them."

Find one person you can tell the truth to.

Tell them you need vulnerability and give yourself permission to show your sorrow out loud and in full bloom. Author and professor Brene Brown say this about vulnerability in her book *Darely Greatly*, "Vulnerability is the core, the heart, the center, of meaningful human experiences." I couldn't agree more. Maybe you have felt in the past that being vulnerable makes you appear weak. I hope you can start to see things differently today and agree instead that strong is overrated.

CHAPTER 6
MOVING ON

Moving on is a simple thing. What it leaves behind is hard.
— Dave Mustaine

*I*t's time for you to move on. Say that to me, I dare you.

Charley was an excellent communicator and, at times, a bit of a controversial teacher. I would sometimes even get a little uneasy when he would speak to big crowds, especially when I first heard him teach about recovery. Why? Because he appeared to me to be, well, a little upset. Maybe wound-up describes it better. His voice would rise in volume, and he would say a curse word or twenty. But this was how he expressed his passion. It bubbled up in him, particularly when discussing subjects like childhood sexual abuse and addiction that were close to his heart. He wanted to help people in such a deep way. He wanted to see people heal.

If you didn't know him, you could possibly mistake his passion for anger, but once you knew him, you would never again doubt how much he cared. Maybe you have a passion like that for something and can relate. I know I can. I, too, can get excited and sound, well, passionate at times about some of these topics. Talking about some of these things smack dab in the middle of my own grief may make me appear a bit zealous as well, but I promise I'm not mad. *I'm passionate.* (Wink, Wink!)

Anger is normally out of character for me, but it's been a reality for me recently. Grief does weird things to us. When I started this book, I believed it would be important to write through my journey, not simply *after* I was feeling relief. I knew this book would, at times, be a raw look at how grief is affecting me in real time.

Like with my journaling, as I look back through chapters, the words and emotions that I've been writing, I see how deeply I have been hurting and how things have affected me. But most importantly, as I reflect, I can see how I have healed. I can see the process taking place and how far I have come. It reminds me of a little sign in my home that says, "I only look back to see how far I've come."

Today, as I write and continue to hurt, I focus on movement. Movement in both the process and the progress of my healing. The progression of our emotional wellness is hard to measure. It's inconsistent. Measuring in and of itself implies there is movement to measure. In suffering, we long to see and feel something happening.

In grief, this movement can be in all directions. Some days I feel I'm moving forward, some days backward. Some days I'm stagnant, motionless.

I realize movement is not rocket science; it's just motion, action. It is a change in the position of something. Movement can be slow. It is often a function of both time and process. As the time passes and the position of the object or, in this case, of the emotion changes, we can say we are undergoing *the process of movement.*

With all of that said, some kind of movement is imperative to feeling differently, better. But as I continue working through my pain, one thing I find difficult to grasp is why people insist we must *move on*. Why has that become a thing? I think it's dumb, and I'm not doing it.

How Do We Actually *Move on* From Something That Happened to Us?

Relationships, pain, love, good, bad, wins, and losses—we can't just snap our fingers and make those memories and emotions disappear. We can't simply act like it didn't happen. I mean, I guess we can, but that's denial, and it will come back to bite us when we least expect it.

Merriam-Webster defines the idiom "move on" as "to continue living one's life in the usual way." Yeah, that's just not possible. Usual way? As if nothing happened?

When someone first said to me something to the effect of, "In time you will be able to move on," all I could think of was, "May I ask exactly what it is that I am supposed to be moving on from? Did I mention my person died? Are you saying that I am now to get on with it? Move on from it, from him?" I am not able to, nor would I want to.

I refuse to act as if nothing happened; or as the dictionary said, "go on per usual."

When I was fourteen, I received a call in the middle of the night that my grandma had been brutally murdered. It was horrific. My Grandma Virginia was a hoot! She was as close to a real-life *I Love Lucy* character as you will find. She looked like Lucille Ball, with a strawberry-blonde updo, and acted like her, too, with her many madcap adventures. She was silly, stubborn, creative, sweet, and caring. My grandma was bigger than life to me. She was young and enthusiastic and did all kinds of fun and crazy things.

But for me, the most important thing about my grandma was that she had a way of making me feel extra special. Have you ever had someone like that in your life? Have you ever lost them?

I am a middle child and the daughter of an alcoholic father. As a child, I cried a lot. I also felt unseen at times. But when Grandma Virginia was around, I felt like the favorite. I felt safe. I've never known anyone else who made me feel quite like she did. I'm fifty-five now, and I think about, feel sad about, laugh about, and generally just croon about my grandmother on a regular basis. I never want to move on from those emotions or from the memories of her.

Let's vow to eliminate the verbiage and hurtful notion of needing to move on. Remember how important words are. Proverbs 18:21 (ESV) reminds us that "Death and life are in the power of the tongue." Words can hurt or heal. What we say matters, so let's change one little two-letter word, the word *on*. We will no longer require or put pressure on ourselves to move on. Understand, I'm willing to move, because motion is required as we heal.

So, as we grieve, we'll keep moving, but not on; forward.

Movement is hard and isn't always consistent or in the correct direction. Sometimes we get stuck; I get that. You may know someone or be someone who appears to be at a standstill. Someone you know may be acting out with behaviors that make you feel like they actually do need to move on.

If someone is stuck, they need help. I never want to dwell on the terrible way my grandma's life was taken. I don't want to think of the details or obsess about the tragedy with Charley. If that was happening for an extended period of time, I would need a deeper look at this obsession, and I would absolutely seek professional help. I saw a grief counselor immediately after Charley died and found it helpful. So, if you or someone you love needs that, please find a professional to help you process right away. Reading books is helpful, but it's not a replacement for in-person counseling or peer groups and community.

We can start moving forward, but don't allow anyone to tell you when or how you should be getting through this. So many people say so many things. I have had to remind myself that most people don't know what to say, and when they misunderstand my grief, I attempt to reply with a gracious nod or a brief thank you.

For those who are my safe people, I may kindly explain how those words make me feel. Anyone who genuinely cares for your well-being will be grateful for your honesty and the education on the correct verbiage. Most humans do not want to cause harm, but this stuff ain't easy. In grief, we understand people feel awkward and weird, so clarity is helpful. This deeper, personal knowledge about caring for others is one little thing I can say I'm grateful for in my grief today. It's a start.

Not long ago, I was talking to a well-meaning family member, whom I love dearly, and they asked me how I was doing. It had been about six months since Charley died, and I replied, "I'm doing alright today, although I'm still very sad, but I appreciate you asking."

The person sounded genuinely surprised and said, "You're still sad?" They might as well have said, "You should move on." Of course I'm still sad! People don't know what they don't know.

The reality is that I'll never not be sad when thinking of losing Charley. The pain is ongoing, surprising, erratic, and mostly silent to those around me. Mourning is hard work, often invisible to everyone but the one in pain.

Our grief is attached to us at the hip but unnoticed by the general public. It's ours, and we must continue to move through it as gracefully as we are able.

Wouldn't it be peachy if we could actually just move on? Thankfully, when we get an emotional punch in the gut by a well-meaning loved one or friend, we can use our tools. We can practice using grounding techniques. Find things that work for you. No one can completely understand what you are experiencing, except you and God. There is no right or wrong in what makes you feel better. Don't be afraid to do whatever it takes to cope, as long as it is not destructive.

I have a beautiful daughter who has some, well let's say, unique dance abilities. Very early in my grief, she was able to bring a smile to the room by being her fun and silly self. I so appreciated finding my smile again watching her. She led a dance-off with my grand-children, and I was thinking as I watched their joy, *I may be able to genuinely laugh again, someday*. I also remember coping by bingeing the TV series *Grey's Anatomy*. Whenever they were stressed or upset (which was every episode) the ladies always "danced it out."

I'm convinced there have been several situations since Charley died that would have been less painful had I opted to go that route, but we know it isn't that easy. Like any other mental health concern or diagnosis, we don't just snap out of grief. We maneuver and move forward through this process at our own speed. Like my daughter's special dance moves, we can respect the quirky rhythm and unique-ness of our grieving.

Remember, we are in the process of moving. No quick fixes here.

Timing is unknown in all of this. In my experience, grief has proven to be a process that's taking much longer than I expected. It certainly caught me off guard. As one who practices good habits and healthy coping, I had no idea how hard this loss would actually be. Much of our roller coaster of emotions depends on the unique relationship we had with the deceased, but it's always surprising how extended the grief journey is. While there is no real timeline, some variables can affect us each differently.

- What were the circumstances surrounding the loss?
- What is your own personal comfort/discomfort with strong emotions and vulnerability?
- What is your support system like?

All these things make your time frame different from mine. You may also find yourself *emotionally constipated* at times or unable to articulate the simplest of feelings. This is very common. Along with the days of uncontrolled crying and outbursts, grief can bind you up inside, figuratively speaking.

After Charley died, I saw a grief counselor who used this metaphor to describe what I was experiencing. You can find it at The Foundation for Loss (www.thelossfoundation.org). I suggest you look it up for yourself, but it describes grief as being shipwrecked, holding on to a piece of debris, and being slammed by waves. The wave size and frequency are unpredictable. On days we think the sea is calm, a wave will surge back again, and it feels as though it will drown us. Gratefully, over time, the waves get smaller and are spaced farther apart.

This accurately describes how I have felt and continue to feel. It spells out how things change and don't change.

In reference to his own journey, Charley used to say, "As I heal, the pain doesn't altogether leave, but I find as I move forward, that I am hurting less often and for shorter periods of time." It's comforting how his wisdom continues to speak to me, even now.

When the waves feel out of control, we can refocus on the truth. Feelings are valid but sneaky. Having strong emotions is normal, and not having emotions is normal. That is to say, as normal as normal can be in this season. I've always liked the quote from author and public speaker Patsy Clairmont, "Normal is just a setting on a dryer." Exactly.

One of my biggest stumbling blocks is how harshly I have judged myself when trying to decipher if what I'm feeling and experiencing is *normal*. As humans, we tend to be our own worst critics. We may judge ourselves harshly for feeling too much, not enough, or feeling nothing at all. There is no handout with the correct number of ups and downs or dos and don'ts on any given day of grief.

I'm grateful for a community of healthy friends and family who told me numerous times that I could stop apologizing for how I was feeling on any given day. Whatever today looks like, keep moving. Six months or six years later, keep going friend.

Healing Takes Time, And No Apologies Are Necessary for the Grief We Feel

Today I am able to see and feel some of my movement. I look back and see that I have actually moved a few feet forward. In the first few days and weeks after Charley died, I hated waking up each day. I'd wake up and remember what happened like I was hearing the news for the first time each morning. The shock and pain and disbelief hit me over and over again like the movie *Groundhog Day*. That feeling isn't completely gone, but it has softened. Today when I woke up, I missed him, thought of him, of us. I was sad as my mind remembered and then I immediately went to, "I smell coffee; must have coffee." I see movement.

It's never going to be the same as before, but it doesn't feel like a nightmare on repeat today.

We have permission to take our grief along with us. We can continue to touch it, feel it, carry it, pull it out whenever the desire is there. It will not leave us or let us forget about it, and in most cases, we wouldn't want to.

However, not all loss is created equal. What if you really do want to forget? Totally valid. If your loss includes a situation or someone you didn't like so much or who hurt you, you can still agree to move forward with positive action. Moving forward is for you, not them. We all deserve to find peace again.

Unfortunately, if someone you know cannot respect that this loss is now a permanent part of your life, you may have to ask *them* to move on. I hope this is never the case, but we must protect our process and our mental wellness. Mental wellness for me means my emotional, psychological, spiritual, and social well-being. Mental wellness affects how we think, feel, and act. It also helps determine how we handle stress, relate to others, and make healthy choices.

Our rhythm is different from others. It's different from our former rhythm as well. Our new cadence, our tempo, and flow are personal. Life plays and sounds differently than it used to. This is not surprising. In fact, God told us long ago in the book of Ecclesiastes 3:1 (NIV) "There is a time for everything, and a season for every activity under the heavens." This journey is yours. It's your timing, your rhythm, your song, your loss, your movement, and it is to be respected.

God continued in Ecclesiastes 3:4 (NIV) to remind us, "There is a time to weep and a time to laugh, a time to mourn and a time to dance." If the urge comes upon you, please don't hesitate to *dance it out.*

CHAPTER 7
ACCEPTANCE

Acceptance of what has happened is the first step to overcoming the
consequences of any misfortune.
— William James

$\mathcal{A}$cceptance is a word casually thrown around. It's common to be told we are going to have to accept this or that. We are told to accept people and situations the way they are, typically because there appears to be no hope of change. Acceptance is commonly used when talking about recovering from trauma, loss, and addiction.

But how can I possibly use this word or apply this principle specifically in my grief? How do we find acceptance in such a painful situation? If I'm not careful, my lack of acceptance can make me feel like I'm failing in my ability to move forward. I don't want to simply accept what happened, therefore I judge myself for not being able to *figure this out* and move quicker. Wrong again, Julie.

Death is a lot more complicated than simply accepting it happened. Acceptance is not a once and done, and it's certainly not giving in or giving up. The school of thought we've heard over the years is that acceptance is the fifth of the five stages of grief. I understand the concept of the stages: denial, anger, bargaining, depression, and acceptance. But, there is no correct order to the grief stages. And these stages come, go, return, and leave at will. The stages of grief are in no way linear or completely understood. They disappear for a day and then jump right back in bed with you again when you least expect them.

I've had times when I believed I was in a place of acceptance, only to fall quickly into a denial stage once again. I have also experienced what I call close "emotional relatives" to the traditional five grief stages, and they stop by uninvited. Some examples are irritability, irrational thinking, morbid sarcasm, uncontrollable laughter, and the list goes on.

In my profession, I have also heard the term acceptance evolved one step further to "radical acceptance." The term is often used in counseling and recovery, particularly when a person is experiencing great pain. It's a principle that I began to learn as I worked on my recovery from alcohol addiction, and now I'm wondering if I can apply it to my suffering in grief.

Radical Acceptance has been defined by New Life Counseling[1] as, "The ability to accept situations that are outside of our control without judging them, which in turn reduces the suffering that is caused by them."

Sounds simple, but is not at all easy. If I really think about this concept of *simply accepting things the way they are,* this can sound like we just put blinders on and walk around in a perpetual state of denial. It can feel like we are willing to be passive in our actions and thoughts. I am not a fan of passivity. Letting things happen and idly standing by when there is obvious action to be taken is a hard no for me.

I don't want to simply go along with whatever I see others doing just to fit in or fall in place. But on the flip side, in my grief, I don't always see an obvious action step to make things feel better. Sometimes there just isn't any relief in grief. So do I sit and wait, perhaps passively or do I choose to radically accept all that has happened? Realistically, even the overachiever in me realizes this is extremely difficult, and I'm going to need time and grace to find acceptance of what feels so incredibly wrong and unfair.

The word acceptance also takes me back to some unhealthy things my dad would say to me as a child: "Do as I say not as I do." This implies that you don't need to know the why, just accept what I told you (even when he did the opposite) and don't ask questions. Or my all-time favorite Dad answer. "Just rub some dirt on it," he would say. Accept it and move on, kid. Yikes.

> In reality, we know phrases like this will not help us to accept anything. We are looking for answers. We want the why. We demand an explanation, but we may never get one, at least not in this lifetime.

Charley often quoted the *Big Book of Alcoholics Anonymous* on page 417, which says this about acceptance: "Acceptance is the answer to all my problems today. When I am disturbed, it is because I find some person, place, thing, or situation—some fact of my life—unacceptable to me, and I can find no serenity until I accept that person, place, thing, or situation as being exactly the way it is supposed to be at this moment." Reading this during my grief, my insides screamed! *"Exactly the way it's supposed to be? This is not how it's supposed to be!"*

I find myself even more frustrated at that statement twenty years sober than I was when I first heard it. Why? Because tragedy continues to strike the innocent, and bad things happen to good people every day, and because, well, people can be jerks. Doesn't this terrible truth give me some justification for being pissed off, mad, sad, sarcastic and a little unaccepting? I'm not sure it *justifies* my behavior, but I know that even Jesus kicked over a table or two.

I don't believe AA or Charley meant to hurt anyone with statements like this. Instead, as I dig deeper, I can assume the writer had a genuine desire for us to realize that the solution to how we may be feeling on any given day can be found in our ability to work on finding some acceptance of our current situation. Yep, more action required. Grief is work. Emotional, hard work.

So I am reexamining acceptance. When AA says *acceptance is the key to all of my problems today*, I believe for my grief it means *acceptance is where I will start to find peace*.

I want, no, I'm starving for, and need some peace. So yes, I am willing to do some emotional work to get a little peace. I am willing to consider a radical type of acceptance if the promise ahead is a "reduction of the suffering that is caused by this pain." A reduction in pain, yes, but is that it?

Unfortunately, not. We must fight the impulse to think that acceptance means we are supposed to be done grieving. If we aren't careful, the concept of acceptance can imply we are done, healed, over it. Before you know it, we'll be telling *ourselves* to move on.

We know better than this by now, but we are also not naïve to complacency. We've seen those occasions when someone really does need to pull up their big boy or girl short-shorts and get to moving. Moving somewhere, somehow, for themselves and their family's sanity. But in most cases, and certainly in grief, it is unkind and unrealistic to imply that someone has had enough time and, well, should get over it.

Getting over something and accepting something are two very different things.

I can absolutely work on accepting where I am today. I can accept that tragedy happened, and in time, I will begin to move forward. I accept all of that, but I don't believe I will ever be able to fully accept that this tragedy was acceptable or exactly as it should be. For me, it wasn't.

Jesus was clear on this topic. He told us life is not going to be fair, and that statement I believe and accept 100 percent. We don't agree with evil, tragedy, terrible accidents or injustices to children around this world, but we can agree those things happen every day. As I've continued to think of accepting my reality today, I have been able to say out loud that *I agree*. I agree this terrible thing did in fact happen; I agree that it is real, but I will never accept that it was okay.

Is it really possible for me to begin working on acceptance as I write this, only six months out from my own loss? I think it is. Will you stay with me while I practice? This is hard.

Practice sound something like me repeating this to myself:

I agree Charley died. I hate it, don't want to accept that this is my life, a life without him in it, but I agree he did die, and I believe that if I don't agree to work on coming to some place of acceptance, I will live my life outside of my desired level of peace. Maybe forever.

It's painful to come into agreement with tragedy. It's work, but we can do work. We will practice acceptance, and in this case, yes, it's radical. Let's return to the definition: "The ability to accept situations that are outside of our control without judging them, which in turn reduces the suffering that is caused by them."

We agree and work to accept that what happened did in fact happen. We begin to visualize how living in a place of peace might feel again someday. This is for our peace, not to make anyone else happy. Acceptance is for us. What happened is unchangeable. We have been forced to quickly come to terms with this reality at a deep level.

It's more specific after loss of life because we know they are gone. There is no hope of reconciliation or progress toward healing a situation. That relationship is gone forever. We know these things logically, but coming to terms with saying I accept this, can feel somehow wrong. Like, oh well, that happened. I guess I must accept this.

Acceptance doesn't mean you've decided what happened is okay.

The acceptance concept is very similar to forgiveness. When I forgive someone's actions against me, I'm not saying what they did was okay. I'm saying I forgive them, so that I might find more peace. Forgiveness is letting myself off the hook, not them. It's about seeking peace. It was stolen, and I want it back. We are on the hunt for peace. It is the ultimate treasure. Acceptance will come if we allow the process to take its natural course.

This is not giving in or giving up. On the contrary, acceptance is a destination, an expedition to peace. It may come quickly and leave again just as fast. Allow this to be part of the process, and you will find your interludes of peace last longer and happen more frequently as you practice.

"We find some person, place, thing, or situation—some fact of my life—unacceptable to me." Yes, I do. I will always find tragedy unacceptable, but in order for me to live in peace, I must accept that it happened. I can come into agreement with where I find myself today. I also accept that I will forever be sad that this happened, but once again, as we accept things exactly as they are, the hope is that we will become sad, mad, and angry less often and stay that way for shorter periods of time.

My world isn't very black and white. There tend to be a lot of questions running around my brain. There is a lot of gray. The issue that I have found with gray is that there's not as much peace there. So, I will seek acceptance that this happened for my own mental health and happiness, but I will never welcome these things or stand by and watch injustice with a closed mouth. I will follow God's example against injustice. See it, speak out against it, maybe kick a table or two, but whatever it looks like, I'll attempt to love, learn, and teach in spite of it.

This is downright hard. Since we have been learning how important positive self-talk is, let's put it into practice here as we wrap up this hard work.

Say this with me. "I will never be okay with what happened. Today, I accept where I am in order to guide me on my pathway to peace. I will remember that I am a work in progress. I will be kind to myself, and I will not judge myself or others." Repeat as often as needed.

Great job! We know that no one can tell you they understand exactly how you are feeling, because they don't. Coming to a place of acceptance is a personal and private journey to your unique destination. James had a unique way of encouraging us in his writing. "Consider it pure joy, my brothers and sisters, whenever you face trials of many kinds," James 1:2 (ESV). The apostles witnessed more pain and suffering than most of us can ever imagine, yet managed to at least write about acceptance in a big way. Like James, I will attempt to be a peace seeker. Still, I don't think I will ever be able to *thank* God for this specific trial.

I will thank God for helping me through it, but until I see God in person, I will always question and wonder why.

One last thing I'll share that has been a blessing and a go-to prayer for me is the "Serenity Prayer." This prayer has helped me over the years through many losses and battles. I pray this blesses your heart and brings you some comfort as you seek your own acceptance.

God, grant me the serenity
to accept the things I cannot change,
the courage to change the things I can,
and the wisdom to know the difference.
Living one day at a time,

enjoying one moment at a time;
accepting hardship as a pathway to peace;
taking, as Jesus did,
this sinful world as it is,
not as I would have it;
trusting that You will make all things right
if I surrender to Your will;
so that I may be reasonably happy in this life
and supremely happy with You forever in the next.
Amen.
— Reinhold Niebuhr

---

1. Pottorff, Jessica. *How to Manage Change in a Healthy Way.* New Life Counseling & Coaching, (2022). https://newlife-counseling.com/blog/how-to-manage-change-in-a-healthy-way

CHAPTER 8
HOW ARE YOU? (TO TELL OR NOT TO TELL)

Most of the successful people I've known are the ones who do more listening than talking.
— Bernard Baruch

*L*ife does go on. In the beginning, it feels so wrong, but we are still here and have to find the courage to step back into the world. As I've progressed past the early months of mourning, it's become more and more necessary for me to start showing up in everyday life again. Everything feels different. It feels wrong somehow to get back to things that once felt simple, normal. People see you for the first time since *it* happened, and it's all very awkward and uncomfortable. No one knows what to say, and this includes us, the ones who are hurting.

As I reentered the public, one of the hardest questions for me to answer was "How are you?" Innocent enough, but it started to be a difficult decision of whether or not to answer that question honestly.

I would often think, *Do you want a real answer?* I would consider things like, is this a person I can answer honestly to? Or, is it someone who needs to hear me say a little one-liner for *their* benefit? It was a strange phenomenon, but there were a lot of folks who I felt needed me to help them feel okay about my loss. This was my ever-present, people pleasing, for sure. But honestly, it was sometimes easier on everyone, including me, to just say something to the effect of "Hanging in there," and give a good ole thumbs-up.

The Question "How Are You?" Came Into Play Early and Often

It's a purely innocent question from purely innocent people. The reality is, people aren't always thinking about what's going on with you. Even after a big trauma, I had to come to terms with the reality that life isn't all about me. In times of great grief, it naturally feels like it is all about us. I found it hard to think of anything else but me. But him. But people have their own lives going on. Everyone is dealing with their own pain.

During this time of such intense pain, we tend to forget that other people are focused and thinking about their own lives. It makes sense to think of ourselves more than anything else, but how do we navigate this when we're hurting so deeply?

It makes sense that during difficult times of healing, we must become more self-focused than usual because right now our main source of care will be self-care. Healthy people must be self-focused to a certain degree in order to function, protect, and survive. No one else is going to care for us the way we can.

A common lie is this: Focusing on self-care is selfish.
False.

Being self-focused doesn't mean you are selfish. The opposite is actually true. Taking care of yourself is the most unselfish thing you can do for those you love. The reality is, we are of no help to others if we are unwell. Becoming self-focused, doing self-care, and working on your mental and physical health are essential.

Self-focus doesn't mean we are inconsiderate to others; it means we are finally and appropriately considerate of ourselves.

In the beginning of my grieving, I decided to tell the truth to people who asked about my condition. When someone would ask me how I was, I would simply say, "Terrible, thank you for asking." I couldn't even manage an insincere "Hanging in there." Some folks would be shocked at my response, but I found most appreciated the truth and agreed that it made sense.

As I got a little better and had more time between me and the loss, I was able to answer differently, but my hope is that you will allow yourself to say whatever you need to in response to "How are you?"

I also concede that sometimes it is easier to just say, "I'm fine." I mostly find this word to be negative because it's not typically an honest response. In my world, there is an acronym for fine. "Freaking, Insecure, Neurotic, and Emotional." I tell my friends, if I say I'm fine, it's likely I am anything but.

But as I quickly learned in my grief, there are always exceptions to my rules. There are folks who may only warrant the *F-word*, because they aren't safe. At times, I don't have the energy for anything else. On those days, I let myself off the hook and decide it's fine to be fine.

When stepping back into what once was our lives, there are other variables as well. We won't always know who we will see ahead of time or what they will say. There is no simple equation to determine who I can trust with my pain and who I can't. My best advice is to be prepared for people to ask you how you are but not really want to know. Keep your expectations low. Be prepared with your pat answer so you can pull it out of your toolbox as needed. For me, I would say something to the effect of, "Some days are better than others" or "I'm making progress" and then I would add a "thank you for asking," because I always do appreciate people asking about me.

Being prepared can help you reduce harm to others, yes, but also to yourself. I've also committed to try to offer others an extra portion of grace during the grief process because, in this turmoil, grace is in high demand.

On the flip side of this coin, may I suggest that if you are speaking to someone and ask "How are you?" don't ask unless you really want to know and are prepared to truly listen. Have you heard of active listening? If you haven't, I encourage you to read more about it and start practicing it immediately in all of your relationships. There is a very important difference between hearing someone speak and truly listening.

Scenario #1: Doctor's Office

After Charley died, I made the difficult decision to move back to Colorado, where most of my immediate family lives. This meant changing everything from the grocery store to jobs and doctors. Everything. When your life is upside down, this stuff is hard to fathom.

Before I made the move, I took advantage of getting done what I could in Ohio. Things like going to the dentist, my yearly checkups, etc. I went to Doctor #1 to get my "lady checkup" about a month prior to moving. I hadn't seen Doctor #1 since Charley died.

When she came into the room, she sat and said hello. And then there it was: "How are you doing?" A typical question from a typical physician. The problem at this point wasn't her question, but her response. I proceeded to tell her my recent story. She was my doctor, after all. Wouldn't it make sense to tell my doctor about my current mental and physical state?

You would think.

I said something to the effect of, "It's been really hard. My fiancé passed away suddenly in a fire, and I've had a lot of ups and downs mentally." I continued to share that as far as coping, "I've been eating sugar like it's crack, and oh, I'm moving across the country. I'm scared and angry. It's been really hard, doc." Tears flowing, deep breath. *Whew, you did it. Good job, you!*

Doctor #1's response quickly followed and went something like this: "Okay, well let's get you up on that table."

What the actual @*^$&#^?

Yep, that's what she said. Get on up here, sister, and let's take a look-sie. Not even an "I'm sorry." No acknowledgment of actually listening to the words I just painfully spoke. Wow, all I could think was, "I'll never do that again."

Thankfully, grief sometimes allows us to go into a denial fog. We move and function without really being aware of what's happening.

I believe it's a God-given trauma response that takes over in moments like these. Shock first, then denial, often followed by anger. Luckily for me (and her) the shock and denial took over before the anger did, because once I left the office and was able to process what had just happened, I was rip-roaring mad!

For me, anger typically looks like withdrawal and crying; this day was no different. I sat in my parked car and cried, a lot. It wasn't the first time, and surely not the last, that I would sit alone and ugly cry in my car.

Charley used to tell me, "Babe, lower your expectations, and you'll be a lot happier." When he first said that, I immediately thought, *Wait a minute, that can't be right.* I do expect a lot from myself and others. I want excellence, kindness, and love in my world! Unicorns and rainbows are part of my scenario. I want everyone to be happy!

The reality is when I place expectations on others or myself and they aren't met, I'm always disappointed. Going into discussions, appointments, meetings, and relationships with lower expectations is a great life hack. On any given day, we don't know what someone has available to offer, physically, mentally, or emotionally. We don't know their story, their mood, or their health. It's not that I don't want good, high-quality, and healthy interactions, but I've learned that not everyone is capable or aware of what is needed or even appropriate for others. I have blind spots. We all do.

This is where we practice our active listening skills. Being intentional about listening has helped me more than I can tell you. I am learning to truly listen to what someone is saying, without thinking about my amazing upcoming answer or advice while they are still talking. If I am actually focused on them and what they are saying and not my phone, thinking about what I want to do later, or how I want this conversation to end, I can be of service. When I simply listen and then respond with only what I have knowledge about, I have a better chance of causing no harm.

Reflecting back what someone says is an important part of active listening. Repeating what you heard shows you truly listened and helps you to process.

We must be mindful about offering unsolicited advice. Most folks aren't seeking a solution, but instead, a friend. More often than not, people don't want your fix but want someone to allow them to speak uninterrupted and without judgment. We all want to feel heard. We may have great experience and encouragement to share, and they may or may not be interested in it.

We must remain open and unoffended when dealing with others' pain. If you're not sure, it is always best to ask if they want your input. Give them a chance to let you know what is needed. But no matter what, we can listen and show compassion by demonstrating we truly heard. Compassion is a key to joy in this life. There are all kinds of humans walking around this earth. Self-aware, unaware, hurting, happy, kind, mean, all kinds. They will respond to you in a variety of ways, and it's up to you to receive what is helpful and let the rest fall on deaf ears.

There is a time to not listen as well. With Doctor #1, I had to let her poor listening skills go. I had to remind myself that on that particular day in that particular office, for her, even though maybe it should have been, it wasn't about me.

Scenario #2 Doctor's Office

Different day, different doctor, different results.

When I moved, I eventually needed to go to the same type of doctor as Doctor #1. I had no recommendation or help, just a Google search and some availability. When I visited Doctor #2, my defenses were up like a prickly porcupine. I was quiet, withdrawn, and just looking for what I needed.

After enduring the new patient rigmarole, I was finally in the room with Doctor #2. I had no intention of being vulnerable this time. She came into the room and asked me some health questions and then proceeded to say, "So what brought you to Colorado?"

Immediately my defenses went up, my heart rate increased, my skin felt warm and clammy. A flashback triggered by the response of Doctor #1. My brain quickly said to my body, *Can we just get outta here?*

I have learned the value of pausing and taking a deep breath. I spoke the truth to myself. *Once again, Julie, she is your doctor. She needs to understand who you are and what you need. You can do this.* I was a grownup woman after all and could use my big girl words, even at the risk of being hurt again. Right? I reminded myself I could and would continue to do hard things.

I proceeded with caution. "Well, since you asked." I laid it all out. My fiancé, the fire, my family, my life, and now here I was, in this foreign land, seeking a doctor who wouldn't be rude and make me want to cut them. Maybe I didn't say it exactly like that.

As I exhaled and looked up, I saw her looking at me with great empathy. Much to my surprise and relief, Doctor #2 had actively listened and heard me. Her first words reflected back the horror of what I had said. She went on to say, "I'm so very sorry for your loss." She appeared genuinely shocked and full of compassion for my situation.

I immediately thought, *Thank you for confirming how shocking and terrible this is.*

She didn't stop there. Doctor #2 went on to say that she and her husband would be praying for me that evening and asked if she could offer a hug. I went outside and ugly cried in my car again, but for a very different reason this time.

Proverbs 18:13 (NIV) says it very clearly: "To answer before listening—that is folly and shame." All people are humans and will prove it every day. If we take Charley's advice and lower our expectations, we may see our level of peace elevate. Being intentional about having grace for yourself and others is a powerful tool for healing.

Expecting people to understand, know or even care about the same things we do is unrealistic. We get to decide who we tell and don't tell, and as we heal, we can choose to offer grace to those who just don't get it.

In the book of Colossians 3:13 (ESV) we are reminded to "Bear with each other and forgive one another if any of you has a grievance against someone. Forgive as the Lord forgave you." I remind myself often, that people can't read my mind any more than I can theirs. Even in our times of pain, we can be gracious and patient with those around us.

This is all so much. It is all so difficult to navigate in the midst of feeling like our world has turned upside down. I understand and want to encourage you as we wrap up this chapter. If you have to interact with other humans today, consider your expectations. Are you expecting too much of yourself? Of them? If you feel like you can't do it, maybe you need a day alone or perhaps your answer consists of "I'm fine, thanks." If your day requires you to interact, think ahead. Pause, pray, proceed. And whether you have an interaction similar to Doctor #1 or Doctor #2, if you need a good ugly cry, by all means, get in your car and let it go.

CHAPTER 9
YOU'RE NOT CRAY-
CRAY ON CRY DAYS

The truth is you don't know what is going to happen tomorrow. Life is
a crazy ride, and nothing is guaranteed.
— *Eminem*

During this exhausting journey, there have been times that I thought maybe I was going cray-cray. This extreme sadness can feel like or mimic a clinical mental crisis, but it's rarely the case. If you are feeling any thoughts of hurting yourself or others, please call a medical professional immediately or dial 911 and tell them how you are feeling. They are trained to assist you and your loved ones in extreme cases such as these. I hope you can remember that you are loved and this pain is temporary, even if it doesn't feel like it today.

How we behave and feel during this mourning period may be confusing for some. Some people may confuse deep mourning with depression. They are not the same. Both offer us great sadness, and both cause disruption in our lives, but the similarity ends there. Depression can be clinical, but grief is not, except in very rare cases. Grieving people are not automatically depressed, but they are intensely sad.

If you feel you cannot make any progress back into life, please ask yourself this question: Are you able to feel more emotions than just sadness? You may certainly be sad, but can you also laugh and find some joy in the things you love? Depression seems to inhibit our ability to experience any positive emotions. It becomes a mental health concern when depression takes over and we think *only* in the negative.

Grief does not. Positive emotions come and go in grief, just as negative ones do. You may be able to genuinely find joy in certain familiar things early on after a loved one dies. It might feel weird and at times even wrong, but it isn't. If you are anything like me, you may even find yourself saying off-color jokes, inappropriate comments, or morbid statements and laughing uncontrollably all the while. This is grief.

I had the sense that a light had been shut off when Charley died.

I was foggy, and everything felt dark inside my brain. It can be difficult to find the light switch again. We may not have the energy or drive to even look for it or the desire to flip it back on, even if it is right in front of us. It is important for us to keep a watch out and gauge our grief state and mourning period to ensure we are not slipping into a depression.

Professional Help is Highly Suggested With Any Significant Loss or Trauma

Extreme sadness can feel as though it will never end when we are in the thick of it. That is not an unusual feeling, but we know grief is a big fat liar. It hangs around way longer than we are told it will, but it does get better with time.

I currently work in a mental health facility, and as such, I don't like the word crazy as a catch-all for mental health. So, for clarity, I only use it to demonstrate my point of grief today. The dictionary currently defines crazy as mentally deranged, especially manifested in a wild or aggressive way.

Grief isn't like that but if we are not aware and intentional about solutions, grief will try to play tricks on our minds.

It will lie to you, tempt you with negative thoughts, encourage bad coping behaviors, and in turn, grief will work to shame you for having those exact thoughts or behaviors in the first place. It's a sick cycle. If allowed, grief can appear to be *driving* us crazy. It's important we continue talking about all of this to prevent long-term consequences of grief.

As time passed after Charley died, there were days and times I could leave the house and be productive and even thrive at work and in social settings. Getting back out there was slow but I was doing it. Leaving the house seemed like the most impossible task in the first few months. Especially the thought of going somewhere alone, without a family member or close friend. I would think:

- How can I drive and stay focused on the road?
- How will I remember what I even went to the store to buy?
- What if I see someone I know and they ask that dreaded question, "How are you?"

There have been many times I have felt mentally unstable in all these scenarios. But this is grief, not insanity. As time passed, it became clear that I was going to move. I gained confidence in being in public and began to consider what mattered the most to me. The answer eventually became crystal clear. I needed to be closer to my family.

Leaving Ohio Was Hard But Necessary For My Healing Journey

Along with the move from Ohio to Colorado came the unwarranted shame of feeling like I had somehow left Charley behind. My emotions ran high. I had brought everything from my home down to the last plant because of my emotional attachments to him, to my old life. I couldn't bear the thought of leaving or losing even one more thing, so I was meticulous about packing every single item I owned. Many unneeded items, I might add, and it's perfectly understandable.

We may feel unrealistically attached to certain things after a loss.

It's not weird or crazy. I felt the need to keep things like a tiny, dried flower from five years ago and an old, dried out eyeglass wipe, for example. Realistic emotional detachment from stuff is also a process and takes time, so don't judge. We will remember that we are continuing to do the best we can with what we have at this time.

After getting through my first Christmas without him and making the road trip to Colorado, my emotions were not as stable as I had hoped for. I was wondering if I was, in fact, going crazy. When would this get better? What was wrong with me? Why was this taking so long? All traps.

One particular day after I made the move, it was snowing pretty hard outside, and I was in a new town, which already had me feeling insecure about driving. Nevertheless, I decided to go run errands. I needed to get keys made for the new house, go to Costco, Walmart, etc. It all began innocently enough, but when I went and started my car, I quickly realized the wiper blades were frozen to the window, so I began to clear the snow from my car. I lifted the wiper blade without a thought, and it promptly snapped right off in the cold. Perfect. I was headed to Walmart for new keys; I figured they would have a new blade as well. Doesn't Walmart have everything?

I attempted to build myself up and put my knowledge into action. I began thinking about what I was thinking about. *You got this, JuJu.* I was determined to be intentionally nice to me on this day and practice all that I have been preaching. I proceeded to pull out of the driveway.

I barely knew what street I was on since I had moved so recently. So, the snow was coming down even harder, and there was no wiper on the driver's side. I had my hand out the window to clear the snow enough for me to drive safely. The road I now lived on was under construction. Oh, and yep, it was official; it was a blizzard. With my other hand, I was attempting to steer and get the GPS to tell me how I actually get to Walmart. But hey, I was F.I.N.E.

When it came to stuff like driving to new places, getting stuff for the car, I would normally defer to Charley. Of course, he would be happy to help me with anything. I missed that. With Charley, if there was a need, he always had a guy. For me, he was the guy.

I accomplished driving to Walmart without a wreck and went in feeling determined with the broken wiper blade and keys in hand. I had already attempted to have keys made twice prior to this trip and they still wouldn't open the door, so to say I was frustrated with the key makers at this point would be accurate. I wanted to get a refund and try something different, but I couldn't get an associate to help me. I was becoming a bit angry. Maybe I was *hangry*, but I wasn't having it. Either way, I was determined to remain *fine*.

I felt myself spiraling a little as I continued to wait at the key counter with no response, so I went to the wiper blade aisle, where I again couldn't find an associate to help me either. The list of blades and all the types and varieties were right there in front of me. You would think a grown woman in her fifties could follow simple instructions and pick out the appropriate wiper blade replacement.

I simply didn't have it in me that day to act alone. Grief had managed to make me feel incompetent on bad days, and that day was a glaring example.

Since no one was helping me, I decided to call another auto store while standing in the Walmart aisle. A kind young man directed me to the correct replacement blade at the store he didn't work at.

I was pretty proud of myself at this point. And without warning, I suddenly felt the need to take a very deep breath. I stopped in my tracks, frozen in the wiper blade aisle. I looked around; I was alone. I looked at the wiper blade, then the keys, and then it happened. The tears just came. It was now completely out of my control. There is no warning siren before this kind of tsunami hits. In the aisle of Walmart, with no advanced notice, I began to ugly cry.

This wave hit hard. I'd say it was conservatively a 200-footer. My brain just said, "I'm done." Why did I have to do any of this without him? Why was I here in Colorado in the first place? Why did I have to figure out car stuff and why in the world was I getting keys to a house that he didn't live in with me?

Why God?
Why?
Will you ever answer me?

Crazy? No, I hadn't actually lost my mind. My mind just hurt. It was broken. I may have temporarily misplaced my mind, and frankly, I didn't have the energy that day to find it. Episodes of grief like this are not uncommon. I understand them better now and accept them as part of my journey. Having had several of these grief events has made me more compassionate and I will even say hypersensitive when I see someone in a public place who looks like they lost their best friend. I can't help but wonder if they actually did.

There is a sacredness in tears. They are not the mark of weakness but of power. They speak more eloquently than ten thousand tongues. They are the messengers of overwhelming grief, of deep contrition, and of unspeakable love.
— Washington Irving

There is nothing to be ashamed of when you find yourself having an incident of uncontrollable grief. With time, we start getting back to life. We have jobs, families, and friends. We have places to go, people to see, things to do. Not if but when you have a flood of emotion unexpectedly take over, be kind to yourself. Sometimes I excuse myself to the bathroom and take a minute, or I might pause and be intentional about allowing myself to feel the feeling. I breathe and give myself grace, no matter who is around or what I'm doing.

On those occasions where there is no control, when it sneaks up on you unannounced and is happening before you even realize the tears are leaving black lines of mascara down your cheek, I encourage you to let it happen. Men, in those moments you may find yourself feeling embarrassed for crying in public or in front of any other human, again, I encourage you to find a way and a place to let go of any old lies about "real men don't cry." Such a sad and unhealthy lie in our culture. Allow your body to do what is needed.

God made tears.

King David wrote it so elegantly in Psalm 56:8 (NLV): "You keep track of all my sorrows. You have collected all my tears in your bottle." What a beautiful image of our Father in heaven caring for us and feeling our sorrow. Let the tears flow, boys and girls, and let the healing begin.

There is a scientific reason people often feel better after crying. Emotional tears are a concentration of prolactin, manganese, serotonin, cortisol, and adrenaline. Yep, a bunch of big words that create a special "God potion" that we need in order to feel better and regain some energy. Most of these substances in this potion have some role in mood and stress regulation. Did you know that humans are the only animals who cry into adulthood? It stands to reason it is one of the ways our Creator designed our bodies to heal. Get it out. You are not a crybaby, weak, or a dramatic person because you cry more than someone else. You may just have been created with a little extra helping of the God potion.

Crying does help, but even so, there have been and, I believe, will continue to be days where I wake up messy in my emotions and unable to manage very well. I will fall into all the grief traps, forget all I've learned, and only want to eat ice cream. When we have emotional dreams, or for me, have been overly consumed with other issues in life that tend to keep us in a bit of a welcomed state of denial—i.e. busyness—we may suddenly find ourselves in the middle of a cry day.

I had one of these days very recently. I went to work, and in a team meeting, I was asked to share an icebreaker about something that causes me to be anxious. Icebreakers are designed to help coworkers get to know more about each other.

I thought for a minute about whether I should say it and then chose to simply speak the truth. I said, "I'm having a bad grief day and just need you all to know that if I look like I'm crying, I probably am, and it's because I miss him. Thanks for letting me share."

It's hard grieving in front of people, but being vulnerable makes it so much easier for those around us to understand and support us.

Don't be afraid to share your why with those who care about you, because the reality is you may periodically have these intense days, these cry days, months, years, and even decades from now. This is a journey of epic proportions. We must not attempt to hurry along this process.

I believe that these cry days are often needed in grief. I notice that after having a period of relative peace, often accompanied by a busy schedule, I have a cry day. I assume because my emotions need to be released. This is healthy. We know it is, because again we find ourselves in good company: "Jesus wept" (John 11:35 (ESV).

CHAPTER 10

FIRSTS AND BEYOND
(LET'S MAKE A PLAN)

Grief is the cost of falling in love.
— Unknown

*W*e've talked a lot about what it's been like to survive the initial shock and early stages of grief. It's been hard, hasn't it? Thank you for walking through this with me. It means so much.

Strange how it feels like this tragedy happened years ago and yesterday, all at the same time. Not seeing, hearing, or touching him all of this time has felt intolerable at moments, and at other times, I've managed to go through days fairly peacefully. It's been almost a year and this anniversary coming up brings me to a place to ponder the difficulty that firsts can present. I don't understand this whole "just get through the firsts and you'll be okay" mentality. Like it somehow makes it all better once we survive the firsts.

The first-first I had to endure was my birthday. My birthday is on the fourth of July, just three weeks after Charley died. I've always loved celebrating my birthday. I always loved the notion that God made me on this one day, and that I get to be celebrated each year! It *is* actually all about me, at least for this one day.

Charley was so excited about this new birthday tradition. He had never celebrated his birthday like I did. I spoiled him rotten and loved celebrating his special day. He would get so excited for my birthday, sending me little gifts and special cards all week.

My first birthday after Charley died was terrible; I didn't want to celebrate anything. I was grateful to my closest family members for making it tolerable, but my heart was so broken. In the beginning, it wasn't simply my heart that was broken, my whole body felt broken. Like so many other days to follow, when I think of that first birthday without him, it's hard to fathom how I was even upright. Humans are so resilient. I remember writing in my journal that day.

I only wrote, *"It's my birthday. You're not here. I'm trying not to be so mad at God. It's not working."*

After my birthday, a lot of other little firsts came. The first time I went *there* without him, did *that* without him. Happy things, sad things. Often a social media post popped up with a memory reminding me of events and happenings. Trips and outings. These have been both precious and bittersweet each time.

Holidays come and go. We anticipate the pain ahead of time, and it causes anxiety and fear. Each first brings its own set of emotional challenges, and often no one else seems to realize it is even happening to us. There are so many firsts that are private or unseen. With time, grief becomes very silent and unnoticed by others.

I can't make more memories, so I will cling to all the ones that are shared with me. I understand it may be counterintuitive, but remembering a story, a saying, or speaking a lost loved one's name out loud means the world to one who is grieving. Rest assured, there is no way for you to make me feel worse about the fact that he is dead.

Talking about him doesn't hurt me, forgetting him does.

Life's Big Events

Getting through big events that were already planned is excruciating. For me, this included my daughter's wedding, just three months after Charley died. Life does, in fact, go on. It feels impossible, but we are required to, or at the very least, expected to persevere through these important and nonnegotiable dates and events.

My daughter's wedding! A day I had imagined for over thirty years. I could never have imagined I would have a huge, pesky black cloud following me around the entire time. I just went into my highest gear possible. I got myself ridiculously busy and was able to avoid any deep conversation with anyone, for the most part. I said things like, "Will you excuse me? I have to do this" or "It's so great to see you, thank you for coming." All the while thinking, *"What can I find to do so I don't have to actually talk to anyone and keep acting like I'm okay?"* I worked like a crazy person during my daughter's wedding and was so grateful for that distraction. I don't know what I would have done if I hadn't been given lots to do.

Once it was reception time and there wasn't much left to do, I had to stop and was forced to see what was in front of me. I needed to be present. I wanted to try to enjoy the beauty and love. When the time came for the father-daughter dance. I was finally forced to stop and observe.

I watched in a daze as my daughter danced with each of her brothers. One after the other, the three of them tapped each other on the shoulder to take their turn and held her tight for their section of the song. Not having a father figure present at that moment was debilitating for my soul. As I watched my boys' love for my girl, I looked around and everyone was crying. A lot of hard crying. It was so emotional. There really isn't a way to describe it. It was thick. I stood there emotionless, like someone who didn't know a single one of them.

Somewhere in the recesses of my mind, little flashing pictures of the years of raising these four beautiful children were trying to show themselves to me. The past five years with Charley were pestering my memory banks relentlessly, but still I resisted. I stood in the crowd of sobbing relatives and watched without emotion like a cold stone. The tears came later, of course. But in that moment, my body, my mind, and I believe my God, knew that if even one tear came, it would open a floodgate of great proportion, and there would be no turning back. As soon as it was over, instead of crying I chose to cope by dancing it out, hard.

Another significant first for me was Charley's birthday. Dear friends came and stayed with me. I'm blessed with great friends and family who like to keep me busy and doing big things, like climbing mountains, during hard times. It really matters.

Following that, it was our anniversary. The week leading up to our anniversary was particularly terrible. The time we focus on the impending *first* can produce more pain than the actual date we are anticipating. Three weeks away from the anniversary of Charley's death I felt completely consumed with it. Thinking about it made me feel so very sad and lonely. It was most definitely a trigger. The actual day was much less difficult than the week leading up to it.

> As we anticipate the firsts, we go to the worst-case scenario. Especially for the first firsts, because we don't have a point of reference.

As we progress and make it through each date, we will see that we do have the ability to navigate through them. *Relief comes from knowing.* Perhaps knowing helps us to feel as though the next one won't be quite as mysterious and scary. It will always be an emotionally triggering day, but we will have some frame of reference.

The truth is, with the loss itself, we have already experienced and survived the worst pain imaginable. It's all difficult, but nothing about this loss will be as hard as that first day, ever again.

Big Year. Big Lie.

A one-year survival doesn't miraculously make everything somehow peaches and cream. People said typical things to me like, "Give it a year, and you'll feel fine." Or "After a year, you'll be ready to date again."

After enduring this for a year, we understand it more, this grief, but it continues to feel terrible. As I went through the one-year mark, I was very sad. I was hurting badly, and it was hard to talk to anyone about how hard it really was. Many had mostly forgotten about my pain by this time.

This first brought everything back for me. It felt fresh to my mind and emotions as if it were all somehow happening again. In my dreams that week, I would be in the house looking for him. I could smell the smells. It was awful. For me personally, it was some of the most excruciating, long-term pain I've experienced. I cried alone that week. I cried with friends that week. I just cried a lot.

It finally came and, just as quickly, it went. So now what? The day after the one-year anniversary, all I could think was, "I made it through all the special dates. Yippee, go me. A whole year without him and now, I have to do it again, and again and..."

There is no time limit or reference point for the letup of grieving. A year doesn't mean diddly about how you should or shouldn't be feeling.

Don't put that kind of pressure on yourself or others. You have some reference points now and some new experiences, for sure. But ultimately it means that your trauma happened a year ago and you are starting the 365-day cycle once more. One day at a time, one date, one event, and one memory at a time.

Seconds will be hard... thirds, tenths, twentieths. I'll never stop thinking of Charley and the memories, the loss, the pain, the love, the joy. Will I think of him, of it, less? I imagine the answer is yes. I really hope so at least, because I do have a desire to heal, but I'm not putting any kind of restrictions or timers on my emotions and feelings. I hope you won't allow anyone to do that to you either. Every person is unique, every situation is its own.

Grief is the Psychobiological Response to a Significant Loss

It affects the mind and body substantially. It sticks around and holds on in the form of an unrelenting yearning. We will never stop being sad about loved ones being gone. We will always miss them. Grief is, in this way, permanent. Permanent, yes, but paralyzing, no. At least, it doesn't have to be.

I find Psalm 34:17-18 (NLT) comforting when I feel no one understands how I'm feeling. Only you and God know the depth of your sorrow. As you read this today, I pray that you might find some comfort from your God: "The Lord hears his people when they call to him for help. He rescues them from all their troubles. The Lord is close to the brokenhearted; he rescues those whose spirits are crushed."

God understands, and I take comfort in knowing he suffered and understands my pain like no one else can.

As you prepare for the upcoming events and anniversaries, consider what will serve you well on these difficult days. For me, it varied. In the earlier days of my mourning, those days were planned and spent alone with those I felt total freedom to be my sad-self. I did not have the capacity or desire to be "on" or available for others. The holidays came, and I stayed quiet. It was painful. Keeping close to family was my salve.

It was not a typical holiday season for any of us, and it didn't matter. I did what I was able to do. In the past, I was usually the host and the life-of-the-party kinda girl. The first year, post loss, everything was too painful. I couldn't care for others when caring for myself was a big enough challenge.

Planning to do very little is a good plan.

Plan ahead and make your needs and wants known to those who are supporting you. This will save everyone some added heartache.

On the one-year anniversary of Charley's death, my closest friends came to visit, and we planned a hike and dinner. It was active, healthy, and healing to be with people who not only loved me but loved him. It was hard, but more tolerable than being alone.

My second birthday after losing Charley, I had a rough week. I asked my closest friends and family to join me, and we did a big physical event that day. Wearing myself out physically always helps my mental state. I climbed my first fourteener that day (14,000-foot mountain), and I kept thinking how he would be cheering me on! He was always my biggest fan, and as I got higher and higher up the mountain, I couldn't help but feel closer and closer to him.

Journal Entry

It's my 2nd birthday without you and the gangs all here to help me endure. We are hiking my first 14-er today babe, you would hate the climb, but love the summit. You always said you felt God in nature, where the air is thin. You would call it your "thin space". A place where you felt closer to heaven than usual. I'll be up real high today, try and touch me, ok? I miss your touch.

This second birthday without him was different. It was by far better than the first. This shows in real time our real hope. We do get better. I was so grateful to have my friends with me on that day. As you approach difficult days, having an idea of what you'll do to cope is very helpful.

Another idea for getting through these special days is serving or helping with something your person cared about. Serving others always gets us thinking less of ourselves. Changing how you look at the day is huge. Maybe it is an intimate time with just a few, some time alone, or a party with as many people as will show up. You get to decide because while it is still about them, it's really more about you now.

I don't want to think about that day and its trauma each year, but I do want to think of him. Tragedy ended his life, but it didn't end our relationship. He will always be someone important in my life. So consider what you enjoyed doing together with your loved one. Charley and I enjoyed baseball games on occasion. It was one of the last events we did together. He loved them Yankees, so going to a Yankees game may be a way to remember and celebrate him in the future. Doing something that brings you joy can flip the script on your grief-laden day. Try different things, ask for ideas and help. This is a lifelong journey for you, plan accordingly.

CHAPTER 11
LOVE MATTERS

$\mathcal{W}$ e've come a long way, friends. Funny how things that didn't matter before matter now. For example, the number eleven has become significant to me. Charley was born on the eleventh of February and died on the eleventh of June. The number eleven mattered to him, and now it will always matter to me.

You, too, will have new things that matter to you. Things you have become very sensitive about and maybe even a bit protective of. These things can take you by surprise.

For instance, I couldn't throw away a little packet with a moist towelette in it. You know the kind you open and use to clean your glasses. Yeah, for the longest time, I looked at it and just held it. Once, I accidentally washed it in a pair of pants, but even after that mishap, I needed to keep it. It was dried up and useless, but it was his. Charley always cleaned my glasses; it was just something he did for me. Oh, how I miss those little things. Keeping this piece of trash may sound silly when saying it out loud, but it's not silly. It mattered until it didn't anymore; at which time I was able to throw it out.

Some people won't appreciate what matters to you now. These new things that matter are between you and your person. They will stay with you forever.

Hold on to them; they are yours, and that's all that matters.

Recently, I made a pit stop at a gas station to see if I could buy a bungee cord. I had been hit from behind in a hit-and-run accident a couple of weeks prior, and my bumper was cracked and starting to hang down.

In the midst of the gas station trip, my mom called. She had been self-cleaning the oven, and it had somehow made the entire house fill with smoke! This wasn't the worst part. Not one of her three smoke alarms went off.

When Charley's house caught on fire, no fire alarms went off. The batteries had not been replaced. This was a trigger. Mom's statement totally freaked me out. My mom wasn't thinking about this being a trigger for me. People don't know or remember what happened in your life 24/7. Don't expect them to.

I immediately ordered three new smoke alarms on Amazon and went into the gas station bathroom to have a good cry. As I walked out, I realized I needed to eat, so I went and ordered some food. I waited quite some time as I stood at the counter wiping back the tears that kept invading my face.

At long last, a girl came to feed me. As she took my order, I glanced at the clock on the wall and noticed it said 11:11 a.m. She stated, "That will be eleven dollars and eleven cents." I said, "Really?" (here come the tears again), and then I shrieked "Awesome!" This outburst was quickly followed by an outbreak of uncontrolled and embarrassing laughter, but I didn't care. That sign was for me, and I knew it.

Another thing that matters to me now are hawks. Charley loved these strong birds of prey and felt a connection to them spiritually. He said when he felt confused or was looking for some direction from God, he would pray, and if he was on track, he believed God would send him a hawk to let him know he was heading in the right direction. I loved his faith and his willingness to share it. Did hawks come to him as a sign from God? Who's to say? He believed it, and that's what mattered. Now I search and ask God to see hawks constantly because it brings me comfort, and comfort matters a great deal.

What new things matter to you? If you don't know, think about it, and keep your eyes open.

God made all creation, so he is obviously able to allow us little signs of comfort from time to time. There are all kinds of personal little signs and reminders that I've heard about from people. Things that remind them of their loved ones and can bring peace and hope. With my loved ones over the years, it's been different things, including butterflies, orange Jeeps, cardinals (red birds), squirrels, magnolias, and puzzle pieces, just to name a few.

Puzzles are recent. Jigsaw puzzles are something I've come to enjoy doing in the past couple years. Not long before Charley died, I was finishing up a large wooden puzzle of a beautiful Native-American woman. Charley did not really care to sit and do puzzles, but he always encouraged me in my puzzling because he recognized it was grounding and peaceful for me.

One day I was working on this particular puzzle, and I was struggling to find two very small, and I mean tiny, pieces. Luckily, patience was one of Charley's greatest traits. That day, and that day only, he agreed to sit with me and help me with the hunt for the two elusive pieces.

As I continued frantically searching, huffing and puffing, he sat quietly and just gazed at the table covered in little pieces. A few minutes later, he reached over, grabbed the two missing pieces, and filled in the two little spots that had been driving me batty. I was so excited and started high fiving him and telling him what a great team we made! I thought after this experience he would surely start puzzling with me, but he never got the chance. Puzzle pieces matter to me.

That same puzzle was barely finished and still on my dining room table the day he died. I had it framed, and soon after that, unexplainable puzzle piece signs started happening.

I was texting with a good friend. Her husband was like a son to Charley, and they have a beautiful daughter who is four and whom Charley adored. My friend texted me the following: "Our girl is missing a piece to one of her puzzles today and she told me, as her rationale, 'You know daddy's buddy in heaven, Charley? I bet he wanted to do a puzzle, so God came and took a piece for him.'"

This four-year-old, of course, had no prior knowledge of why this would matter to me. Frankly, neither did her mom, but it did.

After Charley died, people would approach me and tell me they dreamed of puzzle pieces in reference to me or him. Someone prayed for me, not knowing I was even in the back of the room, and the prayer involved a puzzle and a vision of Charley's hands giving me pieces. It happened several times. No one knew about my puzzle except me and a few very close friends, so I clung to each word and the remarkable statements from strangers and friends alike.

In grief, we can be so overcome with pain and sorrow, we may not be open to other things, like the many little miracles happening all around us.

God doesn't give up on his children. I am so grateful God continued to pursue and remind me of his love even while I was so mad. I'm asking you, even if it's difficult, keep your heart and your eyes open for what I call "God winks."

Today, I am able to give thanks for these small blessings. They can make me smile, cry, ponder the meaning of life and on the best of days, help me feel seen and somehow not forgotten by God.

I'm Starting to Get Better. You Will Too.

I'm feeling consistently and increasingly better most days now. I'm definitely not the same girl I was when I started chapter one. I suppose change is inevitable. Grief changes things. It changes us, our minds, our hearts, our views, and our capacity to love. Have I mentioned, grief changes everything?

I find my view of love has also changed but for the better. I look at people who carry grief, and I can see it. The grief, yes, but also the untamed way they love. I have been so blessed by the memories of the love we shared, Charley and me. It changed the way I live today.

Today, I am not as bitter as I thought I might remain in the beginning. Instead, I long for love and to love those around me. I want every human to experience that special kind of love. I am more and more hopeful with time. Hopeful because of the knowledge that our kind of love does exist. Perhaps it's even possible for me once again. Hard to say out loud? Yes. Can we love the same since our loved one is gone? Who really knows? I felt like my life was over when this first happened. I felt like no one could ever fill his shoes, and I was right. No one can or will come close. Those were his size fourteens and his alone. Things have absolutely changed, but as Jesus reminded us often, through it all, love remains.

No one ever takes another's place. We understand this and know that God made us all unique.

No one took my dad's place, my grandma's place, or my many friends' places. A life cannot be made up for or replaced, but when someone is gone, they can leave behind a piece of themselves for us to use and grow with while we remain.

When I had my first child, I looked at my daughter and thought, *how on God's green earth could I ever love anyone or anything the way I do this little girl?* It felt completely impossible; until I gave birth to that little boy and then that next little boy. Our capacity for loving is huge. I want to love hard, big, and out loud.

Difficult Loss Can Actually Grow Our Capacity to Love

I can confidently say today that I don't take for granted any love I have in this life. I pray I never do. Life is so special and so precious. All kinds of love. That love of a best friend. You know the one who 100 percent totally gets and accepts you? Your ride or die. Or a romantic kind of love that can spark your every nerve and also get on your last one but will always be the person you want to say good-night to and the first person you long to see in the morning.

And be still my heart, the kind of love a parent feels for a child. This love mimicking the love of our heavenly Father to us, his kids.

Grief is the result of love, and because of my experiences with both, I long to treasure life more accurately today. I want to love as God does, relentlessly. There is a cost, but I believe it is worth it.

May our hearts never grow hard or cold, but instead simply continue to grow and expand.

As I ponder these last sentences and prepare to go, I am finding it hard to leave. I'll miss this. I'll miss you.

I desire for you to know and believe you are going to be okay. In the beginning, I couldn't imagine myself here today. I was nowhere near being this girl eighteen months ago. A girl who knows she is going to be able to move forward, and not just limping and broken, but moving with intention and love once again. I long for you to hear, believe, and trust me when I say, *you are going to be okay.*

Your road will certainly be different than mine. It's like selecting the route home on your maps app. Maybe you will be on the fastest and most direct highway. Maybe you will choose the avoid highways option and stick to the back roads. Maybe you don't even need GPS. No matter your route, you will arrive at your destination based on your unique and ever-changing ETA. Time won't heal our wounds, but it does soften the blow. Stay the course.

Life can be gone in the blink of an eye. We are all too aware. It can knock the wind out of you and leave you so wounded you feel like you will never recover. Through it all, the valleys, the summits, and the flat roads we hike along, we can decide to grow and love. Grow better and not bitter. We can grow our capacity to love in both volume and tolerance. Regardless of our circumstances today or tomorrow, we choose to love *more* deeply, *more* often, and *more* better.

We want to be healed, help heal, be loved, and show love to the best of our ability. We want to keep working and keep healing right on through the suck. As the old Chinese proverb advises us, "You cannot prevent the birds of sorrow from flying over your head, but you can prevent them from building nests in your hair." We can choose.

We can decide to pause when needed, pray consistently, and to proceed through the process. We will read and study and seek help if needed, and in doing this, we are choosing to keep those birds out of our hair and in the trees where they belong.

I hope this journey has brought you some solace and you will continue with me as we commit to stay the course as we progress each day toward love, compassion, acceptance, truth, and the steadfast journey from grief to grace.

CHARLEY AND JULIE

ACKNOWLEDGEMENTS

I am profoundly grateful to every individual who has allowed me to share in their journey of grief over the years. It has been an immense honor.

First and foremost, I extend my heartfelt gratitude to my mother, Norma (Nana), for her unwavering strength and constant presence.

To my children: your love, support, and unique qualities have been my pillars of strength. Erin, you are my comfort, confidante, and best friend. Brandon, your encouragement and positivity are a constant source of inspiration. Ryan, you are my stability, strength, and motivation. Brian, your heart and faith helped guide me back to my heavenly Father. To my children in love, Steve, Nichole, Lauren, and Kelly, thank you for standing by our sides.

To my siblings: Greg, thank you for being my refuge and comic relief when it was so needed. Stacey, thank you for showing up, always. Thank you for reading and reading and re-reading.

Ed and Jan, your enduring love and support have been invaluable. Let's continue this adventure.

Julie, Sheila, and Jason, my babysitters, my tribe, my family. Your support and presence have carried me through the toughest times. I can't thank you adequately for coming to me so often and helping me climb these mountains, literally.

The rest of my beautiful tribe: Meghan, Tina, Kara, JBrad, Aubrey, Sommer, Susan, Amy, Amber, Angela, Roxi, Farrah, Carol, Genevieve, Heather, and Cherri. Thank you all.

To my chosen sisters: Alice, Kathy, and Mary. Thank you for keeping me in the fold even after. I'll always choose you.

Daniel, you never let a day pass without seeing me. Thank you for letting me adopt you.

Sue, my wise counsel, you'll always be my hero.

Scott, thank you for loving me right where I'm at.

My extended family, who are too many to name, thank you for continuing to love me. Thank you Sara and Missy for paving the way on this difficult path.

Pastors Paul, Jeff, Kevin, and Seth. Thank you for teaching me about Jesus. My extended church and CR forever family. Your presence and love have been a constant source of strength and love.

To Cheryl and Laura, thank you for taking a leap of faith and starting Grief's Healing Choices. And my group of ladies from GHC. Your understanding and support have been invaluable in navigating this journey a week at a time.

To Stephanie and the team at the emPower PR Group, thank you for believing in and seeing this project through to completion.

To Jesus, thank you for never leaving me, even in my darkest moments. This book is dedicated to you.

ABOUT THE AUTHOR

 Julie Maguire is a former business executive, ministry leader, and Nationally Certified Peer Recovery Supervisor hailing from Denver, Colorado. With a rich tapestry of experience, Julie has become widely recognized for her expertise in serving, leading, and educating on the recovery process. Her passion lies in facilitating mental wellness, both within secular and non-secular contexts.

As a communicator and teacher, Julie draws from her extensive personal journey marked by triumphs, trauma, and spiritual growth. Through her work, she empowers others to navigate their own paths towards healing and wholeness, emphasizing the transformative power of healthy choices and a deepened relationship with God.

Despite the gravity of her vocation, Julie is affectionately known as "JuJu" by many, embodying a delightful balance of warmth and whimsy. Infusing humor and silliness into her approach, she believes that laughter is an essential ingredient in the recipe for resilience and restoration.

With a tender heart and a lifetime of experiences, Julie possesses a unique ability to guide those around her toward a more loving and healthful perspective, even in the midst of life's challenges. Learn more at julie-maguire.com.

www.ingramcontent.com/pod-product-compliance
Lightning Source LLC
Chambersburg PA
CBHW070720130626
46553CB00005B/2083